# Why Economies Rise or Fall

## Professor Peter Rodriguez

**PUBLISHED BY:**

**THE GREAT COURSES**
**4840 Westfields Boulevard, Suite 500**
**Chantilly, Virginia 20151-2299**
**1-800-TEACH-12**
**Fax—703-378-3819**
**www.teach12.com**

ISBN 1-59803-658-0

# Peter Rodriguez, Ph.D.

Associate Dean for International Affairs
Darden School of Business,
University of Virginia

**P**rofessor Peter Rodriguez is Associate Dean for International Affairs at the Darden School of Business at the University of Virginia. He received his B.S. from Texas A&M University and holds an M.A. and a Ph.D. in Economics from Princeton University. Since 2008, he has also served as a trustee of the Darden Foundation. Previously, Professor Rodriguez was a Lecturer at Princeton University and a Professor at Texas A&M University. He also served on the faculty of Semester at Sea and has taught in universities around the world.

Professor Rodriguez is a practicing economist and specializes in the study of international business and economic development. He is also an active researcher whose current interests include the interaction of globalization, economic development, and social institutions; the consequences of corruption for multinational corporations; and seed-stage finance in emerging markets. He has published research on international trade policies, firm investment patterns, the measurement and effects of corruption, and practice-based studies of issues in international business.

Professor Rodriguez worked for several years in the Global Energy Group at JP Morgan Chase, where his assignments centered on work for multinationals such as Royal Dutch Shell, Pennzoil, Apache Corporation, Enron, Santa Fe Energy Resources, and Halliburton.

Professor Rodriguez has extensive experience as a keynote speaker for academic and corporate conferences and in executive education. His private teaching engagements include work with the AES Corporation, Harris Corporation, Rolls Royce, and Visa.

Despite his many activities outside of the classroom, Professor Rodriguez remains a teacher at heart, and his many teaching awards include the University of Virginia's University Teaching Award and Mead/Colley Award for Engagement with Students, as well as Princeton University's university-wide Teaching Excellence Award. In the fall of 2009, Professor Rodriguez was named one of *DiversityInc* magazine's Top 100 under 50 in America. ∎

# Table of Contents

# Table of Contents

## SUPPLEMENTAL MATERIAL

## CREDITS

Data provided by Angus Maddison.

# Why Economies Rise or Fall

**Scope:**

The fundamental basis for all economic theory and policy is to improve living standards and promote stable, generous societies. Every abstract construct and each impenetrable phrase describing deep concerns over the balance of payments or deflationary expectations is designed to offer sensible guidance on how we can and should manage our private and public affairs to make life better. Economics is the science that aims to make the most within our sometimes dismal limits, all the while acknowledging that to do so requires that we work cooperatively and freely. Much of economics, however, reflects the complexity of our world and the limits of a science that must rely heavily on history's natural experiments. We live in the laboratory of economics, and from it, we observe firsthand the struggles and successes of nations pursuing the same fundamental objectives.

This course examines the large lessons from experiments using different strategies and ideologies for economic growth. From these experiments, we will gather insights into what makes economies successful, strategies that often lie hidden beneath the larger banner of a particular theory or set of beliefs. In short, we uncover the roots and secrets of economic growth from the successes and failures of many nations over the past two centuries. In this effort, we learn how economies work and why some countries grow quickly and others don't. The course offers the context and skills needed to properly discern economic successes and appreciate the objectives and challenges facing all those who seek to ensure the stability and richness of their nations. The course examines the most successful economies in recent history, including the United States, Japan, the Asian Tigers, China, and others. We also study economies that have experienced a combination of success and failure, such as the former Soviet Union, Vietnam, and India, as well as some economies that have struggled mightily but not grown, such as Nigeria and Venezuela.

To understand the challenges of growth, we must also ask about the constantly evolving nature of our economic and physical environment and whether growth can persist. The issues of "instantaneity" and a hyper-connected global economy rapidly consuming key resources are significant though not entirely new obstacles to the quest for continued growth. We also examine longstanding challenges to economic success and societal cohesion, including corruption, poverty, and inequality. Understanding how these issues connect to the larger fabric of economic ideologies and policy making delivers a fresh perspective on key issues facing the global economy. Among the most important of these is an understanding of how economic and financial hegemony may change with the rise of China and the deep structural issues facing mature Western economies. We will examine the challenges of financial and economic integration and what they mean for key economies around the world. From and through all these issues, this course distills the nature of economic growth in a world where so many of the secrets of economic success remain elusive. ■

# From Free Markets to State Economies
## Lecture 1

> Governments aren't really the protagonists in the story. ... People are, in fact, the only ones that run an economy, the only ones that make a choice and make a difference. Policy is all about behavior. Understanding behavior is understanding growth, and that's the direction we're headed.

W e hear about different and often-complicated economic policies frequently, but the basis of all economic policy is to raise the standard of living—to make people's lives a little better. In this course, we'll look at various recipes for growing the economic pie to see if we can identify any that really work.

One of the problems with policy is that it's always rooted in some argument, and the argument is always based on some economic theory. The theory is just a story that tells us the way things are supposed to work. Such stories are rooted in a semi-scientific approach to studying what has or has not been successful and under what circumstances. The bases for economic theories are the "isms" we all know so well: Keynesianism, classicism, Marxism, libertarianism, and so on.

This course distills lessons we have learned about economic theories, in particular, economic theories of growth, from the broad set of growth experiments that have been undertaken around the world by both leading and lagging nations. Our goal is to go beyond the stories and ideologies to learn what really leads to growth.

Throughout most of the 20th century, much of the discussion about economics was based on the dichotomy of the Cold War. This first lecture is about dispelling the notion of that polarized economic world and painting a more honest picture of economic development.

In the end, what we're interested in is not what economic courses different countries have taken, but which ones have succeeded and which ones have failed, noting, of course, that all of them have experienced both success and failure. To really get behind the story of what works in an economy, we have to set aside the isms. Good economics is all about incentivizing productive behavior. It can come in many forms and in many circumstances, but that's the only thing we need to remember. The appropriate environment, however it's constructed, makes productivity profitable. What we'll learn is that there are many paths to economic success.

> **One of the hard realities of this is the truth … that macroeconomic policy and growth theories are not scientific. They're just not. They're scientific-ish at best.**

To understand the story of economic growth, we have to understand how well different economies have fared over the years. To do that, we need to look at the numbers and the stories behind the numbers. The United States, for example, has been the most successful economy in the world for the past 100 years, but the average growth rate for the U.S. economy over the course of the 20th century—a period that saw a number of wars, the Great Depression, and a wide variety of economic policies and precedents—was just about 2 percent per year. In fact, all the wealthy economies of Western Europe have also grown at about the same slow and steady rate. In this course, we'll look at the forces and policies that influence that growth around the world, in countries from across the political, economic, and sociological spectrums. ∎

## Suggested Reading

Keynes, *The General Theory of Employment, Interest and Money.*
Sachs, *The End of Poverty: Economic Possibilities for Our Time.*
Smith, *An Inquiry into the Nature and Causes of the Wealth of Nations.*

## Questions to Consider

1. What are the distinctive characteristics of capitalism?

2. How different are the overall economic policies of the United States and the European Union? What about China and Japan?

# From Free Markets to State Economies
## Lecture 1—Transcript

Hello and welcome to the course. I'm Peter Rodriguez, and I'm an economist and professor at the Darden School of Business at the University of Virginia. I've been an avid traveler all my life and every time I travel the same question creeps into my mind. I start thinking why is life so different in this country than in the country I just came from or in the countries I've visited in the past? A lot of times the most compelling questions have come to me when I've seen people who didn't lead lives that were so good, even though they were spirited, intelligent, ambitious, thoughtful, even though the geography was wonderful and the place was beautiful. Understanding differences in living standards, where they come from, and what the human-made element is in determining those living standards has been a nagging question for me for at least 20 years. Answering that question and all the questions that relate to it are a big part of this course, and it's something that I'm going to enjoy talking to you about over the next few lectures. So let's go ahead and get started.

We think about economic policy all the time—every election year, almost every day in the papers, cable television, on the radio—we always hear about this policy or that policy. They all seem different and complicated and sometimes difficult, but the truth of it is, there's only one basis for all economic policy, just one thing. That one thing is to raise your living standards, to make people's lives a little bit better. Ultimately, that's the only reason one should study economics or listen to what it says. Ultimately, economics is about not just growing the economic pie, not just making the economy bigger and more successful for some, it's about growing those slices of pie and the slice that everyone gets. We want to focus on that in this course and think about all those policies that are intended to affect those slices of pie and what they mean for us.

We can start by asking ourselves a question: What do we really know at the end of the day? What do we know about economic policies? Do we know which ones work and which ones don't work? It doesn't seem like it. I hear a lot of discussion and not a lot of answers, but we do have some things that we know and we're going to discuss that in this course. We want to discuss whether or not we really have a recipe for growing the economic slices of pie that all of us live on and that we hope that our children will live on and that we hope will grow larger and bigger and a little more tasty over time. That's a big part of what we need to understand with policy, but to begin we need to sort of distill through the fact and the fiction. One of the problems we have with policy is that it's always rooted in some argumentation, and the argumentation is always based on some economic theory. What are economic theories? Economic theories are just stories that tell us the way things are supposed to work. They're presumed causal relationships. The basis for these theories are these "isms" that you know really well. You've heard of Keynesianism, Classicism, Marxism, Libertarianism, and lots of other isms to be sure. But, what are they really?

If you think about an economic theory, it's really a story that's rooted in a scientific approach, a scientific approach to studying what has been successful or what hasn't been and under what circumstances. It's just a story, in some sense. What we do is we take these scientific approaches, and we couch them in these broader stories about economies that have done well, about successes or failures, and through those stories we have the roots of these theories. The problem is it's really hard to separate truth from ideology when you're hearing a story about what objectively has been proven to work and what just seems right or what sort of fits better with another politician's belief or with some person's predisposition towards one thing or the other.

What this course is about is distilling all the lessons that we have about economic theories, in particular economic theories of growth from the broad set of growth experiments that have been undertaken around the world by the leading and the lagging nations of the world. If you think about it, when you think about all the history of the world, these are just experiments. In fact, they're the only experiments economists really have. Studying those histories, what happens in China, Japan, the United States, Great Britain, etc., that is how we learn and that is what we are going to do. [We're going to] look at all these histories, look at what policies have worked there and why, and think about our future. We want to learn what really leads to growth, not the stories and the ideologies, but what's really behind raising living standards around the world. What's really behind eliminating poverty, making a better life for people, and just perhaps possibly a more improved and more peaceful world.

One of the hard realities of this is the truth of it is that macroeconomic policy and growth theories are not scientific. They're just not. They're scientific-ish at best. What do I mean by that? What I mean is that there's no real experimentation. If you think about actual science, you think about controlled experiments. You have a complex set of forces affecting one organism, and you control for every one of them except for one. In the other experiment, you tweak that one variable, and you can study that over and over again under a variety of circumstances to see what really works and what doesn't. The problem with macroeconomics is you just can't do that. You can't take a whole economy and run experiments. You just can't learn that way and it doesn't and we don't; therefore, macroeconomics is just scientific-ish, it's science-like. To be sure, there are a lot of good scientific experiments in and around economics, particularly microeconomics or the individual choices and decisions that you and I make. But, on the macro scale, we're really wedded to these histories and their stories, and so it's vital that we study them and it's vital that we explore them.

It's easy to slip from a world of careful observation about what really has happened to identities about what must be true, or even personal opinions and subjective interpretations of what's happened. In some sense, what we really need to do is think about economics more like we think about astronomy. Astronomy is a science to be sure, but you can't really affect the variables and you can't really run experiments on them either. That's how we think about macroeconomics, looking at these supernovas in history, these black holes of economic disaster, and learning from them the best that we can.

Throughout most of the 20th century, much of the discussion about economics and about what was good or wrong in economic theory was based on this dichotomy, a Cold War dichotomy, of us and them. The us, for the most part, would be in my view the United States, and a free-market open-economy sort of capitalist view of the world. The them, or the state view of markets, would've been that pursued by the Soviet Union where you didn't really have free enterprise. You had a central governing body that made economic choices about what was produced, what prices were charged, and who got what. In some sense, that really polarized the world of discussion about the way that economies worked. The truth of it is, it's not so black and white. That's really an oversimplified story. In its extreme, it's actually probably just not true or a lie. All economies are a little bit less stark black and white than those 2 economies that we learned about.

This first lecture is about dispelling the notion of that polarized economic world and beginning to paint a more honest sincere landscape of economic development. Once we look at that more objective landscape, we can begin to understand differences in small ideas, differences in economic ideology and theory that really make the differences. When we look at that landscape, we're going to see a number of things. The first point I'd like to make is that we're going to see lots of variation. If you look all throughout the economic history of the 20th century and even before, you really won't see black and white stories. You're going to see lots of gray, everything in between. I'd go so far as to say that today the United States and all the economies of the world are all in between. No one's exactly free market, open economy, and no one is exactly state led. Everything is in the middle, and that makes our job a little bit tougher.

To take an obvious example, let's just think about the United States. The United States sort of talks about itself, its own self-discovery and histories about an economy that is very open, very free, rooted in entrepreneurial spirit and Horatio Alger stories. But, in fact, it's always pursued a somewhat mixed approach between a very free-market open-economy view and something where states and governments got involved in different ways. Just think about the United States before, let's say, 1913. Before 1913, you had no federal income tax, you had no Federal Reserve Board governing the money supply, and you really had limited control of prices or anticompetitive practices. The world looked very different. You had no social security. Today we have all of these things, all of these interventions. The world, in fact, looks a lot different in 2010 than it did in 1913 (or 100 years before). That is because the United States has followed a mixed approach and has always looked throughout for different tweaks and different ways to manage its economy.

Think about the Soviet Union. We think about the Soviet Union and immediately we're thinking about a world devoid of private enterprise where the state makes all decisions, but that's not really true. The Soviet Union as well experimented with free enterprise at the margin, particularly late as it was struggling economically. We can look at it and understand that it too has been in the middle and is moving more toward the middle, more in between.

Perhaps the chief example of being in the middle, in between the extremes of perfectly free and perfectly state-led economies, is the European Union. Gradually since the end of the Second World War, the European Union has moved from being more open and more free to having more state interventions. It moved from being a small confederation of loosely connected countries to the European Coal and Steel Community to the European Union, and it's now becoming more of a one-size-fits-all economy where goods and services and even people flow freely back and forth. If we think about Japan, Japan is part state-led, very active, very active government involvement in what is produced, who produces, who's going to compete, how many firms compete, but it's also very free in other parts. One thing's for sure, the Japanese economy has taught us a lot about growth. It's one of the best growth stories of the 20th century and something we'll discuss later in the course. Think about China. It's almost impossible to understand China. It's something almost completely without definition, completely new. It's a capitalist economy, almost über-capitalist, super capitalist, but it has these deep socialist characteristics and a communist backing behind a lot of the ideology that runs it. Is that really a new way to run things? Is it different? It's hard to say.

What we really want to know at the end of the day is not just what economic courses different countries have taken, but which ones of them has succeeded and which ones of them has failed? If we ask that basic question, I can already give you an answer to that. Which ones have succeeded? Which ones have failed? All of them—all of them have succeeded in some ways, and all of them have certainly failed. The United States has had tremendous successes. In some ways, it's the poster boy for economic success over the last 100–150 years. But, it's had market failures that we need to understand. Certainly at the other end of the spectrum, the Soviet Union with its very state-led centralized government had spectacular failures, but even it had some successes that are worth understanding a little bit more.

Because of this dichotomy, because of this not so black and white story and the fact that some economies succeed and some fail, and in fact, everyone of them do, these headline ideologies, these isms about monetarism, Keynesianism, statism, etc., they don't really help you. They're really too coarse of a definition to help you distinguish the winners from the losers. What we really want to understand is what successes all these mixed approaches have had? We can consider just a few to sort of whet your appetite.

Let's think about Japan again. If you want to think about an economy that's been successful, you need to think about Japan because from the end of the Second World War when that economy was absolutely devastated until about 1989, Japan set the world speed record for growth. It was growing at an extraordinary pace, so fast it generated a huge amount of paranoia around the world. Did Japan have some secret, some understanding of the way economies worked that really transformed its ability to become the largest, most advanced, most successful economy? We all would have thought so. In fact, if you look around the world in the late 1980s, you would've thought that Japan was headed to be the world's largest, most successful economy. Then, the ultimate unthinkable happened. That large economy that had had more successes than any other entered into a terrible period of losses and recession and malaise. It really challenged our understanding of what led to economic growth. If Japan had the secret, it didn't have all the secret. It only had enough to last about 30 years. Since then, it's fallen back to earth in the more normal economic performances that we've become accustomed to.

Think about China. Certainly there's no more successful story of economic growth in the late 20th century than China. It's been absolutely incredible, but also heavily centralized, run very tightly at the government level with hard choices about what's going to be produced and who produces it. Hong Kong, before China, was just as impressive. In the freest economy on earth, it couldn't have been more different than China, and yet their performance was almost exactly the same. How do we reconcile these differences? They are very different approaches and still great successes. It must mean we have more to understand.

We can think about Europe the same way. European economies, particularly Western and continental European economies, stagnate or grow slowly throughout the 1970s and 1980s, but they've also achieved a lot less economic inequality. The difference between the haves and the have-nots in Western Europe is a lot less than it is in the United States and other parts of the world. What does that really mean? How about the United States, really the largest economy in the world for the last 100 years? It's fared mostly well, even as it has markedly changed its level of government involvement in the economy. Back in the beginning of the 20th century, the United States had almost no federal government whatsoever, but by the end of the 20th century, it would have a huge federal government. What does that really tell us? If that economy, one similar economy, same geography and same culture, has performed well throughout market changes, how important were those changes to begin with?

That brings me to a point that I think is really important. To really get behind the story of what works in an economy, to understand what makes them work, what policies are successful, you've got to forget these isms. It's not that they're not valuable, but thinking in terms of Classicism, Keynesianism, Monetarism, it really just clouds your judgment. You think of that as a complete story, but it's not. Really what we want to know, really the main takeaway is that good economics is all about incentivizing productive behavior. That's it. Good economics incentivizes productive behavior. It can come in many forms and in many circumstances, but that's the only thing you need to remember. The appropriate environment, however it's constructed, makes productivity profitable. That's the number-one goal of economic policy: Make productivity profitable and, in fact, make it more profitable than all the alternatives. If we understand how to do that, and a lot of the economies have stumbled on it or make it happen, we understand exactly what it takes to make growth a reality and to make lives get better year in and year out.

What we'll learn is that there are many paths to economic success, and they're all largely tough. Governments aren't really the protagonists in the story. It seems like they are, but it's really the people behind the economies. It's really incentivizing their behavior that matters because, at the end of the day, economic growth and all economic policy is just about changing people's behavior. People are, in fact, the only ones that run an economy, the only ones that make a choice and make a difference. Policy is all about behavior. Understanding behavior is understanding growth, and that's the direction we're headed.

What's next? One of the most important things we can do to understand the story of growth and to understand what makes some economies successful and others not so successful is to just understand how well they fared over the years. To do that, we need to look at the numbers and the stories behind those numbers, to understand where has performance been strong, when has performance been strong, where has performance been weak, and what do we think the causes are? Once we lay out that landscape, we'll have a basis for revisiting it with a sharper eye, with new tools, and with more details about what makes some economies successful and some economies not so successful.

To do that, one of the things we can do is to think about the performance of the world's most successful economy for at least the last 100 years, and that's the United States' economy. Something you may not know is that the United States economy is the largest economy in the world at the end of the 20th century, but it was already the largest economy in the world at the beginning of the 20th century. Just how big was it? To do that, what we need to do is define a few terms and to think about that performance over the years.

Here's how we'll start. If we think about not just the size of the economy, which is gross domestic product—that's the value of all final goods and services produced in an economy in a given year, that's the size of the economic pie—if we don't just think about that, but we divide that whole pie by the total population of the United States, then we would get gross domestic product per person or GDP per person. The way I like to think about it is if you think about GDP as the pie, then GDP per person is just the average size of the slices. What we can do is take that number, this metric for the performance of the economy over years, and adjust it for inflation. We want to make sure that we don't have any problems of understanding why your grandfather says that a Coca Cola used to cost a nickel, but now it costs $0.95 or $1.25 in a vending machine. We want to take out the effects of inflation, so that we can compare apples to apples for at least the last 100 years.

If we do that, here's what we'll find. If we look at the United States' economy at the beginning of the 20<sup>th</sup> century, we'll see that the average income level for Americans was about $5,000 per person. That may not sound like a lot, but $5,000 per person would've made U.S. citizens the richest people in the world. Citizens of Western Europe—Great Britain, France, Germany—they all lived pretty well also. Their average income levels weren't much lower, but at $5,000 in 1900, the United States was a pretty rich place. How did that income level begin to change over time? The first 28 years or so were absolutely terrific. The United States economy went from having an average income level of about $5,000 to an average income level of about $7,000. Again, that might not seem like much, but that's about 40% growth over about 25–28 years. It was a pretty good couple of decades for economic growth, some of the best on record in the United States.

Then, as we all know, something pretty difficult happened. Beginning in 1929 and lasting for a number of years, the United States went through its worst economic period. It was the Great Depression, and the United States economy actually grew smaller and so did those slices of pie. The average slice of pie for Americans shrank from about $7,000 per person all the way back down below $5,000 per person in only about 5 or 6 years. What does that mean? It means that for 28 years the U.S. economy grew well, and that everything was lost after that. The United States economy went back to square one, and nothing was quite the same.

The Great Depression is something we'll study in depth, and it lasted an awful long time, but it didn't really end until the Second World War came along. When the Second World War came along, the U.S. economy was boosted almost immeasurably, and it surged out of the Great Depression going from an average income level of about $5,000 per person all the way up above $12,000 per person. That level began to dissipate at the end of the war when production ended, when all the debt that the United States incurred to fight the war, to build the armaments of war, to aid in the reconstruction after the war were ended, the United States regained its path, and the United States economy went back to a sort of normal growth rate. At the end of the day, by about 1950, the United States average income level was about $10,000 per person. Now we can sort of sum up again from $5,000 per person to $10,000 per person over about 50 years. Over the next 50 years, it would go from $10,000 per person to almost $30,000 per person, a really extraordinary growth path for the world's largest and its leading economy over that period of time.

That's a lot of data and it's a lot to remember and a lot to think about, but we can simplify in a way that will be useful not only today, but as we also talk about this concept in future lectures. What I'd like to do is to tell you that the average growth rate over that entire period that seems different, that seems invaded by war and Great Depression and all sorts of economic activities and policies and precedents, it all boils down to a really simple and pretty mundane growth rate of just about 2% per year. For about 100 years, from 1900 to the year 2000, the United States economy grew average income levels by just under 2% a year. Year in and year out, that's all there was to it. Not a lot of fits and starts, not a lot of great surges of supernormal growth and huge slowdowns, the story of the United States' growth, the story of the world's largest and leading economy, is really one of slow and steady—2% per year for about 100 years. We all know about the magic of compound interest. If you do that for 100 years, you get an economy that grows relatively well and living standards that grow relatively quickly.

That's how we think about it. Living in the United States, we tend to think about tomorrow being a little better than today. We tend to embed in our minds when we think about our income levels and the way that we live and the way that we think our children will live, this idea of growth. The truth of it is the 20th century proved that to be more or less true. About 2% per year worked, and it's the story of growth in the world's leading economy.

Interestingly enough, it's also not far from the truth for most other economies. When we think about the United States, we think about it being really different in some sense from a lot of Western European economies, but in fact, it's really not very different. Except for the Second World War, which admittedly is a very big and different event depending on what country you lived in, most of the economies of the Western European nations and of the West in general grew at about the same rate, not a huge difference. If the United States was growing at 2% per year or just under, then Great Britain and France were growing very nearly at the same rate. The differences that occur in these countries today, the differences we see in their average living standards, are mostly explained by differences we saw at the end of the Second World War. Apart from that, they all have the same slow and steady growth story—not very exciting, not very crazy, not very supernormal, just slow and steady.

In fact, you could add in all the countries of Western Europe. You can think about Austria, Denmark, France, Germany, Canada, the United States, the Netherlands, Italy, throw them all in the same pack and what you'll find is it's as if they were dancing to the same rhythm, running to the same beat. All those rich economies grow at a very slow and steady rate. That's what growth looks like in a mature developed economy. It's not based on fits and starts, and the differences aren't nearly as stark as what we're told. The differences are actually relatively minor. What really matters are differences that take place over long periods of time, and there just isn't much to be said for that. In fact, we might think about how wide these differences are and what that really means. If you think about the United States and its spectacular economy, its leading economy over the 20$^{th}$ century, we might ask just how different is the performance of the U.S. economy from the performance of all the other Western European economies? We're always comparing it to Western European powers because of their differences in beliefs, their policies and their cultures, but how different are they?

The truth of the matter is, if we run this thought experiment, we'd see they're not very different at all. Think about the United States economy and think about it this way. Suppose that in 1900, instead of growing at 2% per year over the 20$^{th}$ century, it grew at only 1% per year. If the United States economy grew at only 1% per year, not a lot of difference, then by the end of the 20$^{th}$ century, it wouldn't have been the richest economy in the West or in the world, it would be the poorest economy in the West. That small difference, that 1 percentage per year, that's the difference between night and day in terms of economic growth. That's how small the variation is and that's how narrow the differences are. When we talk about economic policy and we talk about what makes it matter and what makes it important, we're really talking about small nudges that last over a long period of time. At least, that's the story for developed economies. The difference between 1% per year and 2% per year is where all the action is, and that's what all economic policies are targeted at, thinking about how to make that tradeoff.

To begin you might always ask yourself is that an important tradeoff to make? Would I be willing to give up 1% per year of economic growth in order to have other things that might matter more to me? Is growth the only objective that I'm worried about? Maybe I'd rather have more security. After all, you could have a lot of growth, but be really worried about how you're going to live tomorrow or 10 years from now, or really worried that the factory at which you work was going to close and your town was going to collapse. Maybe that security is worth that 1%. Or, maybe it isn't. Maybe it's not a tradeoff we really have to make and have to think about. Maybe we think about that 1% and think it's worth it; over a long enough period of time that difference will really mount up. I want my children, I want my progeny to have a better life, and for that we'll take whatever risk comes along with that extra 1%.

That might mean not just greater risk about how we live tomorrow, but even greater inequality. Maybe my life could be markedly different from the people that live down the block. Maybe we'll have to live with more poverty and more wealth and the conspicuous joining of these 2 cultures and these 2 living standards in one economy. That's really what this 1% is all about. When we think about developed economies, when we think about living well, and when we think about living in rich places and in not so rich places, the difference is really small when we think about the difference between the West and all the economies that reside within it. It's something that we'll want to discuss, we'll want to discuss in terms of the economic policies and the, yes, ideologies and isms that back up those policies.

When we think about economic policy and we think about growth, we need to think about the birth of growth. This story of economies getting richer year in and year out really isn't an age as old story. In fact, it's a relatively new story in terms of economic history, but it's one of the most important events in economic history. It's what's made the difference between some people living good, magnificent, happy lives where they could make choices and not have the physical stress, the emotional stress, not have the physical threat of not having enough resources on which to live or on which to feed their children. It's one of the most important events in the economic history and yet we still don't know how to replicate it. We know that it exists. We see the economies in which it's worked. We can understand their histories and look and exactly replicate their policies, and we still can't replicate the results.

The consequences of this are really profound. The consequences for economic growth are profound, and this course addresses all of these questions. What exactly are the forces and policies that have influenced growth and living standards around the world and over time in countries from all along the political, economic, and sociological spectrums? Can we understand them so well so that we can make lives better everywhere and not make some of the mistakes of the past, not endure the Great Depressions or the Great Leap Forwards, and all the great tragedies of economic history? Can we do this in such a way as to make sense of all the rhetoric that bombards us every day about economic policies? I think we can. In this course we're going to start taking the first steps forward. I hope you'll come along with me, and I look forward to all these discussions with you.

# A Brief History of Economic Growth
## Lecture 2

In this lecture, we learn more about growth and what works when it comes to growth. Which policies succeed and which ones don't? But before we can ask that question, we have to define success. In baseball, a range of batting averages serves as a measure of success: 20 percent is terrible and 40 percent is almost impossibly good. The story of economic growth is similar in that understanding the boundaries is key.

How fast is fast for an economy to grow? Angus Maddison, an economic historian from Scotland, helps answer that question. According to Maddison, an economy that grows faster than 5 percent a year for 5 years or more is truly remarkable. That's a benchmark for **gross domestic product**. If we think about **per capita GDP**, growth of 4 percent per year for 5 years is remarkable. The median growth rate for the 150 or so developed and undeveloped economies around the world is only about 2 percent. Putting these ideas together, we can say that growth at a rate of above 3 percent per year in **inflation**-adjusted terms is relatively fast; growth at a rate of less than 1 percent a year is very slow.

Looking at 5-year windows in the 20<sup>th</sup> century, the countries with standout growth rates and GDP per capita are Japan, Ireland, South Korea, Singapore, Hong Kong, and Botswana. Interestingly, if we look at fast economies in the 19<sup>th</sup> century, the list would be almost the same. The Western economies—the United States, Australia, Canada, France, Germany—all experienced relatively slow growth in the 19<sup>th</sup> century. Note, too, that it's difficult to identify patterns or similarities in the list of fast-growing economies. About one-third of the 150 countries we're looking at are on the list of the slowest-growing economies. Here, too, identifying patterns or explanations is difficult.

We should note three overall considerations in talking about growth and the difference between fast- and slow-growing economies. First, the path to riches is not a single path but many paths. There is great variation, for example, in the slow, steady growth of the U.S. economy and the surge experienced by Japan toward the end of the 20th century. Second, growth is a recent phenomenon. In the West, the set of forces determining economic growth is, perhaps, 150 to 200 years old, and for most of the rest of the world, it's 50 or 60 years old. Finally, growth—or the lack of it—has produced rising inequality around the world. This isn't a story of the rich robbing the poor, but of the rich gaining far more in growth and income than the poor ever had to lose.

> **As it is in other areas of performance, we see that the difference between fast and slow [in economics] isn't nearly as big as you might think.**

In comparing early economic winners—the United States, Western Europe—to more recent ones—Japan, South Korea, and so on—we can see both similarities and differences. First, each of these economies (with the possible exception of Hong Kong) has a very mixed approach—neither fully capitalist nor fully state-led. Second, unlike the early winners, most of the recent winners experienced rapid growth over a short period of time. Finally, the new winners seem to break the classical economic rules that guided the Western economic growth miracle, beginning with the Industrial Revolution. ∎

## Important Terms

**gross domestic product (GDP)**: A measure of a nation's economic activity; the total value of all goods and services produced in an economy in a given year.

**inflation**: A situation of rising prices for goods and services.

**per capita GDP**: GDP divided by the total population of a country.

## Suggested Reading

Diamond, *Guns, Germs and Steel: The Fates of Human Societies*.
Grossman and Helpman, *Innovation and Growth in the Global Economy*.
Helpman, *The Mystery of Economic Growth*.
Kindleberger, *The World in Depression*.

## Questions to Consider

1.  What precise measures can be used to establish that an economy is significantly more successful than average?

2.  How fast would the United States need to grow and for how long to be considered successful at delivering economic growth?

3.  Which countries are the best economic performers of the 20th century?

# A Brief History of Economic Growth
## Lecture 2—Transcript

Welcome back. In the last lecture, we really set the scene for this deeper dive into what economics or at least what macroeconomic policy should do and which ones work the best. If you recall, we talked about the fact that the sole basis for economic policy was ensuring that we would have higher living standards year in and year out. We use that terminology to say economic policy should be about growing the size of the slices of economic pie that each of us have as resources from which to live. In fact, if that's the basis for policy, we then begin to ask a lot of other questions like, which policies work the best and how can we tell the winners from the loser? Can we use these categories, these categories like isms—Capitalism, Keynesianism, Marxism, etc.—can we use these as a guide? I begin to say that actually the world's a little more complicated than that. What we have to do is look at the actual data, look at the evidence, and to take this global tour of economic development and economic activity at least over the last 100 years or so to try to understand what policies have worked well and which ones have not worked well and why they worked well.

Today we want to take a deeper dive into that. In this lecture we want to learn more about growth and what really works when it comes to growth. What policies succeed and which policies don't succeed? But, before we can ask that question, we actually have to do something that's really fundamental and that's just to define what is success. It's really fundamental in any scientific endeavor. You have to know what's the measurement. How do we know success from not success? Be clear about the terms and your measurement and then we can make these assessments. That's really not so easy to do. At any scientific endeavor, and certainly in our quest to understand growth, the first step should be to understand the problem. Why is it that there's growth in some places? Why is it that some economies do well and some do very poorly? The next problem we have is to understand how to measure that growth? How can we tell the winners from the losers and when an economy's doing well and doesn't work well? It's really fundamental to any scientific pursuit.

One of my favorite quotes actually comes from Lord Kelvin of the famous Kelvin scale for temperature. Lord Kelvin wrote: "If you cannot measure it, you cannot improve it." To some degree, he's absolutely right. In order to improve economic well being, in order to raise living standards and understand the policies that allow us to do that, we must first understand what's our measure of success.

Another thing we should always do in any scientific pursuit, and certainly in this one, is to always ask did that policy work? Without evidence—theories, isms, policies—they're just hypotheses and suggestions, perhaps even bad ones about what works and what doesn't work. Oftentimes, a policy that's really favored, an ism that really holds true, is one that just captures the right emotional tone. It seems just or validated or important or perhaps consistent with one's beliefs or perhaps consistent with one's beliefs about what makes them different from other people, from other countries. But, we have to get beyond that. We have to get behind that and ask what really works. Did that policy actually do what it purported to do? Did it meet its objective? For that, we still need that measure of success, and we always need that critical eye.

The basic problem is we have to understand performance before we can tie policy to successes and failures. We have to at least understand the differences in performances to enough degree to be able to say that was good or maybe that wasn't so good. We can get a look at times when things went bad and say, aha, this is clearly a lack of success, an economy that's stagnated, that's failed. We can look at the policies that were in play, we can look at what was taking place, we can get a sense of what was working and not working, and then begin to decide that maybe the secrets lie in that set of policies. By the same token, we can at least identify those instances, those economic superstars and say, in these economies, here's where the growth really took place. These were the ones that succeeded. This is when they began to succeed, and this is how long it lasted. We can at least start to try to understand what it was that led to those successes.

But, until we have some measure of success, we really don't know who to look at. We really don't know who to emulate or what countries to emulate, what policies to get behind and which ones to toss aside. In fact, that's one of the most difficult problems we'll have. It goes back to this lack of ability to experiment. It goes back to this lack of scientific-ness. It goes back to this scientific-ish nature of macroeconomic policy. That's a problem that we continue to have in understanding macroeconomic policy, when we have success and when we have failures.

We could always ask ourselves, would you know good growth when you saw it? I'm sure we've all had these discussions. Someone's going on and on about this economy or that and what made it really successful or not successful, pointing to a leader, pointing to an ideology, pointing to the way they did things back when and saying that was good. But, what is good? How do we define economic success, and how should we define economic success? That's really important, and it helps us understand winning and losing in a very important way. The way to see that this is important is to maybe think about some useful analogies.

One of my favorite useful analogies is to think about baseball. We all understand that in baseball, whether you're a fan or not, a player with a high batting average is a good player. That's what you want to copy; that's who you want to be. But, what is a good batting average? To begin you may want to know what's a batting average, and it's actually really simple. It's really just the percentage of times you get a base hit with a zero added onto it. For example, if you stood up to the plate and half the time you got a base hit, or 50% of the time you got a base hit, we would say that your batting average was 50 plus zero, .500. A player who hits the ball 50% of the time has a batting average of .500 and a player who hits the ball 10% of the time has a batting average of 10 plus zero, .100. It's really pretty simple. But, what's good in baseball?

Actually, what's good in baseball might surprise you. A batting average of .200, a player who gets a base hit only 20% of the time, is really considered terrible. That's the infamous Mendoza Line, below which no major leaguer should sink lest they be relegated to the ranks of those who should have never played the game, who weren't worthy of wearing major league stripes and gloves. Those players batting below .200 are the bad players. But, if we think about it, only twice as much, if you bat twice as high at a batting average of .400, that's nearly impossibly good. In fact, the last player to do that did so in 1941. No one has managed to repeat that fate since. In baseball, we think about the range, and it helps us understand success. The range in baseball is 20% is terrible, 40% is almost impossibly good, and even that's so far away from perfect that it makes the game sort of interesting. The range in baseball is really somewhere in between. You're going to find a similar story with economic growth.

We can look at other examples like sprinting. Sprinting in the 100 meters is a very time-honored tradition at the summer Olympics. A time of 10 seconds for 100 meters would be so fast that virtually no one in the world can run that fast. About 99.99% of the population can run the 100 meters only in more than 10 seconds, but everybody in the Olympics must run it in less than 10 seconds or else they're not excellent. What's really excellent depends on the context.

You can think about cars the same way. Some cars sell for $100,000, but even at $30,000, most people will consider that a car is getting to be a little bit expensive. Understanding the boundaries is really important. Even think about height. If you have someone and it's an adult male and he's 5 foot tall we'd say well, he's not tall at all, but someone twice as a high, well that's nearly impossible—10 feet tall, there's no one on record that tall. Understanding the range is important, then we can understand what's the difference between fast and slow, between tall and short, between a successful batter and not, and certainly between a successful economy and not a successful economy.

Let's get right at it; let's answer that question. How fast is fast for an economy to grow? To get an answer for that is surprisingly difficult, but we have a great assistant. He's one of the best economic historians of all time, Angus Madison, a Scottish economist. His words, his writings about fast growth and about the economic history of the world, are really the economic gold standard. They're the standard by which all growth statistics are measured, and we're going to refer to those throughout. If we consider that gold standard of story, that gold standard of economic success in this supreme history and of growth, we'll think about his numbers.

If we think about economic growth and we think about Madison's numbers, what we'd quickly learn by looking at the history of virtually every economy over the last 150 years, is that growing faster than 5% a year for 5 years or more is truly remarkable. That's easy to remember: Faster than 5% for more than 5 years puts you in the A+ category of economic growth. Almost no economies do that. Right away we have a benchmark from which we can judge—5% for more than 5 years is truly extraordinary. That's only thinking about gross domestic product or the overall size of the economy. If we want to think about gross domestic product per capita—and that's certainly what we want to think about, not just the size of the pie, but the size of the slices—we would even say that 4% per year for 5 years is remarkable. That sounds actually kind of slow, but 4% a year for more than 5 years means you're fast. It's the economic equivalent of batting about .350, and that truly is extraordinary.

If we consider the entire distribution of economic growth from all the countries that we think about, the 150 or so developed and not so developed economies, we'd see that the median growth rate—that is the growth rate that separates the top half from the bottom half—is only about 2%. That 2% really separates the top half from the bottom half, and it's interesting because it's also about the rate of growth in the United States. For the period of the 20th century, the United States is really kind of an average performer in terms of its overall level of GDP per capita; it's a very consistent one though. If we think about the standard deviation, then that's about 0.3%.

You add these things together and what it really boils down to is this: When we want to look at GDP per capita and answer the question how fast is fast, I would say above 3% per year in inflation-adjusted terms is actually pretty fast. We can begin to look at those economies and think what did they do right? What did they have? What's their secret? If we look at the same set of countries, we would say that growing at 1% per year in inflation adjusted terms or lower, is reasonably slow. Certainly something less than that, less than 1% a year, is very slow. We would want to look at those economies as well to try to understand what it was that they didn't do right. What's the source of their failure? What made them slow in that sense? That's really the difference.

As it is in other areas of performance, we see that the difference between fast and slow isn't nearly as big as you might think. In fact, the difference is only about a percentage or 2 per year, but that makes all the difference. Then we can begin to ask, who's really made it, who's really successful, and who's really not? Now that we have defined success, let's look back at the history of economic growth and see who are the real winners, who are the most successful, and who are the least.

If we look at who are the fastest growers, and we use that window, what's the 5-year window for growth in the 20th century, what are the fastest economies looking at 5-year periods of growth, here's the list we would come up with. I wonder if you know who might be on this list. If we look at the 20th century and we look at 5-year windows, those economies with standout very high growth rates and GDP per capita would be Japan, number one, really the fastest growth story and something we want to think about. Japan really sets the mark by which most other economies are judged even late into the 20th century when economies like China are taking off at similar and at sometimes higher rates.

Ireland is another economy on that list. Ireland's an interesting story because for so much of the 19th and 20th centuries, we think about Ireland as an economic lagger, but really it's not. Certainly in the latter part of the 20th century, Ireland embarks on this wonderful trajectory of growth. We want to understand that for a couple of 5-year windows in the latter part of the 20th century, Ireland is a rock star of economic growth.

How about South Korea? That one probably also makes most lists. If you think about it, we think about growth, we think about the Japanese example, and we also think about the Korean example. In South Korea much like the story of Japan in the '70s and early '80s, there was remarkable growth. Looking at their story is something that we can all learn from—a story that closely in some ways emulates the Japanese story, but it's also actually rather different.

Singapore makes the list. Singapore, one of the most extraordinary economies on the planet, a tiny little city-state that was a fishing village of almost complete insignificance 50–60 years ago, is now one of the wealthiest, advanced, technologically sophisticated and safest economies in the world. It's a very different approach and there are lots of different regulations around that economic growth and what made it work, but Singapore makes the list for super fast growth in the 20th century.

Hong Kong as well makes the list. Hong Kong is interesting because, much like China may set the stage or may sort of take the crown for being the fastest growing heavily state involved economy, Hong Kong is one of the fastest growing economies that also makes the list in an almost completely different ideology. It's completely devoid of state-led growth, really the closest thing we have to a real free-market experiment—and it's Hong Kong.

The last one I'd add to the list I bet surprises most, but it would be Botswana. Botswana has this spectacular story of growth much like Singapore in the late 1940s–early 1950s. It's almost insignificant, not on anybody's mind, and certainly a very poor, profoundly poor, economy. But, late in the game, late in the 20th century, it embarks upon a remarkable growth path, the likes of which very few economies have experienced. It's truly extraordinary.

If we think about the fastest of all time, and we think about not just fast economies in the 20th century, but in the 18th century, we might think that we'd have to include economies like the United States or Great Britain or France or Germany—because after all these are the richest economies in the world, or at least they have the largest slices of the pie, the highest GDP per capital. But, the truth of the matter is the list would be mostly the same if we looked at last 100 years of growth or if we looked at the last 200–300 years of growth. The growth patterns are markedly different. These early adopters, the early winners, the Western economies of the U.S., Australia, Canada, France, Germany, those rich countries, actually they grow relatively slow. Even in the 19th century, growth is slower than it is in the middle part of the 20th, and certainly not nearly as fast as the fastest of all time, which would be that list I just rendered—Japan, Botswana, etc.

If you think about this question and we ask who grows really quickly and who doesn't grow really quickly, we might ask is there some pattern that we begin to see? Think about that list again: Singapore, Hong Kong, Botswana, Ireland, Japan—are there any patters in those? Any similarities? Do you listen to that group of names and think, aha, the answer must be… I don't think so. I don't think you see any real patterns there that are obvious at first glance. I think there are patterns there that aren't so obvious that we have to get behind and underneath, but not so many, except perhaps for the early Western economies. Those economies, the economies of the United States and its counterparts in Western Europe, actually do seem quite similar in some ways with regard to the rule of law, their economic policies, particularly about openness and government involvement, at least early in the 20th century and certainly in the 19th century. But not a lot of patterns after that, and that's something we really want to understand.

What about the slowest economies? That's a depressing story to tell, but in fact the list is very, very long. If you recall earlier in this lecture, I mentioned that a slow economy was one that grew at slower than 1% per year when adjusted for inflation. In fact, about a third of the economies and all those that I looked at, all the 150–160, grow at about that rate. Growing slow isn't a rare event; it's actually depressingly common. We might begin to ask, all the variation there, all the variation among the slow growers, what's true? What's true about Nigeria and Venezuela? I think the first thing that would come to your mind would be rich and natural resources, particularly oil, which would seem to be fantastic. It's economic oxygen. Everybody needs it, but in fact those are some of the slowest growing economies of the last half of the 20th century. What gives? What explains that?

When we think about slow growth, we probably should think about China because for centuries China grew remarkably slowly. It went from being what I would say was probably one of the richest economies in the world to, in the early 1960s, certainly one of the poorest in the world. What really explains that and the vast turnaround that they had in the late 1970s and throughout the end of the 20th century? It's difficult to understand, and the similarities aren't so clear. We can even look at the Former Soviet Union and all the economies that collapsed and nearly went through absolute economic turmoil with starvation and the like in the latter half of the 20th century. Some of them were the fastest growers in short periods of the middle part of the 20th century. This is a complex story to tell. There's lots of variation and the headline about this economy or that doesn't help as much as you might think.

If we want to think about growth and we want to think about fast versus slow and we want to think about what makes the difference between this diverse motley group of fast-growing economies and this diverse equally motley group of very slow growing economies, we can think about at least 3 big takeaways. Here's one—it's kind of simple: The path to riches is not one single path but many paths. There are many ways to get from poor to rich or to get from well-off to remaining well-off. There doesn't have to be one approach. It can't be just state-led or just open and free market. We might argue about which one of those might be faster (and we'll discuss that in later lectures) but the truth of it is looking at the actual performance of economies over that period of time doesn't really help. The path to riches looks very different for very different countries at very different points in time. Being somewhere along the spectrum doesn't seem to matter nearly as much as we would've thought if we'd just focused on headline ideology in the rhetoric that we hear when we talk about economic history.

For example, think about the U.S. pattern. The U.S. pattern of growth, again, is a very slow steady almost mundane pattern. There are great surges like the surge around the Second World War, the boom of the 1960s, the boom of the middle '80s. But, for the most part, the average growth isn't much different than 2% per year in per capita GDP. It's a very mundane slow and steady path. That's one pattern. Now think about the Japanese pattern or the catch-up pattern. Let's focus on that just a minute because the Japanese pattern is really remarkable. At the end of the Second World War, after the great devastation that that economy experienced, its per capita income levels were only about 1/4 of that of the United States. It was about 25% of the average income level of the average American. That's what the Japanese had at the end of the Second World War. Then, 25 years later, they had come up to almost 2/3, nearly 80%, of the income levels of the United States and would very nearly catch it by the end of the 1980s. There's a growth period that is 4 times as fast as the average for the United States. It looks very different.

If we just compared the endpoints and looked at rich economies at the end of the 20th century, we'd see the Japanese, we would see the United States, and we would see 2 very different paths, so we don't have one single path, one way to success. There are very different ways. If there's anything that they have in common, it seems to be this: No matter how fast you grow, no matter how long a path or slow a path you take to get to the lead, to the head of the pack, once you make the head of the pack in terms of high-income levels, growth tends to slow down markedly. It doesn't matter if you're Japan-style, state-led, heavily active rapid growth or if you're the U.S., mundane 2% a year, every year, a hundred years in a row. Growth at the top seems to be much slower.

If we think about another takeaway we could say this: Growth is really a very recent phenomenon. We think about it as if it always must have existed, as if all the way back in antiquity, parents thought about a better life for their children, as if policymakers always had 5-year plans or economic growth policies. But, the fact of the matter is, growth just hasn't been around that long. Growth in terms of the West is maybe 150–200 years old for the really exciting levels of growth, and for most of the rest of the world, if it's even been there at all, it's the last 50–60 years. That's extraordinary. This set of forces that have come together to transform lives like no other really hasn't been around that long, and so we haven't really been able to study them that long and understand them at the depth and the level that would seem to merit the importance that they have in the world.

In fact, we could say that we saw nothing broad and big outside of England until the mid-19th century when we began to see growth take root throughout the rest of Western Europe and in the United States. Most worldwide growth is just only 40–50 years old. All the great stories, the economic phenomenon of Asia, the economic phenomenon in China, and the great stories scattered throughout the world are really stories of the last 50–60 years, so it's a recent phenomenon. Whatever lies behind growth is something that occurred relatively recently.

A third big takeaway: Growth, and the lack of it, has produced rising inequality around the world. In fact, we could say without question that inequality around the world and income levels is greater than at any point in human history. The haves have much, much more than the have-nots have ever had before. This disparity really challenges us in a moral sense, in an ethical sense, but certainly also in an economic sense. What does it mean to have a world in which the differences between rich and poor can be so stark? Where we can have people who can live so fabulously well with almost no effort it seems, and profound poverty, grinding poverty that seems indestructible, that seems ever-present, enduring, nothing we can get rid of? How is that possible? Is it evidence that we really don't understand the recipes for growth or that we really don't have the will to spread the secrets of growth around? Or, is the problem just simply that complex?

I can answer a few of these, or at least allude to some of the things that I think are important when we think about inequality. It's certainly true. Economic inequality is profound, but this isn't a story of the rich robbing the poor. There's a really simple reason for that. That is that the winners, the rich, have earned far much more in growth and earned far much more in income than the poor ever had to lose. The story is really a story of growth. Growth is producing inequality. Growth is the story behind it. It isn't a story of theft, at least not exactly and everywhere. It's a story of growth and it being present in some places and not being present in others. You can even think about China. There we have great and fantastic inequality today, but only because there's been so much growth that some have been able to get remarkably wealthy while others have had the wealth pass right over them. We'll spend a lot of time on this and on the story of economies where growth never seems to visit, on the story of why growth seems to pass over economies even when their neighbors flourish, even when all that's behind economic theory that should describe the path to success, even when recipes are present, growth never visits some economies, and we want to understand that. It's one of the most important mysteries that we have to discuss.

Let's compare the early winners to the recent winners. If we do that, and we think about the early winners—the United States, Western Europe—and we think about the recent winners like Japan, South Korea, Hong Kong, Singapore, Botswana, and Ireland, we'll see a couple of similar things, a couple of takeaways that we can have. One of them is that there are mixed approaches. In each one of those economies, except for perhaps Hong Kong, there is a very mixed approach. That is to say that in each of these successful economies there has been neither a fully free-market capitalist open society approach nor has there been a state-led government active approach. Neither one of these polar opposites seems to have produced great success. All of the successful economies we look at are at least somewhere in the middle. Most of them are grouped toward the free market end where we've had greater openness and where we've had greater freedom of economic choice and some reward for entrepreneurial activity, but in fact even that isn't so true. There has been great diversity in economic success. Back to the old pattern that we saw earlier in the previous lecture, success resides throughout the economic and political spectrum.

A second pattern we could see is that the recent winners, that is, those that have occurred in the latter half of the 20th century, really don't look a lot like the early winners. The growth stories of Singapore, Botswana, and the like, really seem quite different. Those are catch-up stories. Those are stories of economies that went from very poor to very rich over a really short period of time, where growth isn't the same old United States 2% per year—it's 8% per year, 9 and 10% per year, for 20–25 years. Where an economy that was falling behind and far behind the lead of the pack suddenly surges to the front, and once it reaches the front it faces the headwinds that are undefined and somewhat mysterious that seem to slow down economic growth. We have this story of catch-up, and we have this story of always in the lead. Those seem to be the 2 stories of great economic success.

are some things similar about them, but they're not strict similarities, a lot of variation, and that gives us ample room to explore, to see what's really behind all those variations. Surely there's more to it. There's something central, something behind those stories that really tells us what is behind growth and what is behind the success that hides behind different ideologies and isms. The new guys, if we think about these new winners, seem to break the old rules, and that's a hard thing to live with. When I think about the old rules, I think about classical economic rules. Classical economics really refers to free-market economics without government intervention, a world in which prices are allowed to vary up and down to let the market clear, so that supply always meets demand. If you have unemployment, wages fall, and suddenly there are new jobs. If you have inflation, prices rise, demand falls, and suddenly the world is back to equilibrium. That's a free-market classical economic approach. Let the free enterprise system take control. Let the free market use its invisible hand to guide the economy towards productivity.

The new winners don't seem to follow that approach nearly as strictly as did the old ones, and there's something in that. There's something about that story that we need to understand. When we talk about those old stories, when we talk about classical economics, we're really telling the story of the Western economic growth miracle. We're focused on the growth miracles of the 20th century; those are the ones that reside in our minds. We think about China, maybe Ireland, Hong Kong, Singapore, South Korea, but really there was a more profound miracle that preceded that. That's the miracle of the Western economies and their success through the Industrial Revolution. That story is one of the most profound and interesting stories in all of economic history, but what is it really? What's behind their successes? What was it that really led the world to invent the idea of economic growth to begin with?

That's such a profound story, the lessons are so deeply embedded in all we think we know about economics and all we have read and learned over the years, that we seem to not even question it. In fact, that's a story that's worth investigating for in that story we see the seeds of our baseline. We see the seeds of the frame in which we interpret all of economic success and failures, and that's the story to which we need to turn. That's the story that contradicts common sense. That's the story that aggravates and frustrates and the story that challenges us. That's the story that demands much further investigation and a much deeper understanding of just what lies behind economic behavior and the successful growth stories of the past 20th century and of the 19th century.

# Economic Growth and Human Behavior
## Lecture 3

**If you remember nothing else about economics and nothing else about this course, remember this: People respond to incentives, … and that's what makes economic behavior change and that, ultimately, is what leads to the differences between successes and failures.**

We've already seen that economic policies or schools of thought aren't necessarily helpful in explaining the difference between successful and unsuccessful economies. The real question we need to ask is: What makes people change their behavior in ways that lead to economic growth?

The fact that people respond to incentives is the driver behind economic behavior change and, ultimately, what makes the difference between success and failure. The **free market**, for example, is a story of incentives. In free markets, you reap all the benefits and incur all the costs of your actions.

Several factors must be true for free markets to work. First, economically productive behavior must be more profitable than the alternatives. Second, a tolerance for risk must be present to enable entrepreneurial ventures to get off the ground. Third, people must have trust in the system and in others. Even when these factors are present, however, things can go wrong, primarily because human beings are in charge.

Most productive economic behavior requires coordinated action from many individuals, but one of the bigger problems in coordinating economic behavior is getting human beings to trust one another. If we can get past that problem, it's gratifying to note that success tends to beget more success, but this natural momentum can also work in reverse. During the Depression, for example, people in general seem to have lost their confidence and their willingness to take risks. Getting people to break out of such cycles is one of the hallmarks of a good economy. The good economies we've seen, with all their diverse ideologies, were somehow able to generate that seed of confidence.

A big problem behind predicting when economic policies will work and when they won't is, simply, that humans are humans. They don't always act predictably or rationally. They're also skeptical; they want to see success before they make a commitment. Macroeconomic complexity doesn't account for these root connections.

In the end, policies aren't enough. Even if we were to enact what we thought were the best policies of the leading economies of the world, people would have to believe in the policies for them to work. That's at least part of the reason why we see both success and failure in such a broad spectrum of economic stories. We also know that sometimes, success can be so driven by momentum that people can begin to take it for granted and not really scrutinize its source. That's the problem that seems to lie behind economic **bubbles**, bursts, **recessions**, and depressions.

**Humans are human, which means that they don't always act in the same way. People don't always do things that are predictable. They're not always logical or rational. They're also not likely to believe you just when you say something.**

The fundamental sources of economic stability and growth are the ones we see at the level of the individual. We see success in free-market economies because people begin to act productively and take it for granted that they should act productively. At the same time, the framing of economic policies in time, culture, and place is paramount. To understand macroeconomic growth, we have to go to the individual level and ask: Why did that policy work with that person at that place and at that point in time? ■

## Important Terms

**bubble**: Rapid expansion of an economy, followed by an often-dramatic contraction.

**free market**: A system in which business is conducted according to the laws of supply and demand, without government intervention. Participants in free markets reap all the benefits and incur all the costs of their actions.

**recession**: A period of reduced activity in an economy.

## Suggested Reading

Gambetta, *The Sicilian Mafia: The Business of Private Protection.*
Helpman, *The Mystery of Economic Growth.*
Keynes, *The General Theory of Employment, Interest and Money.*
Landes, *Revolution in Time: Clocks and the Making of the Modern World.*
Smith, *An Inquiry into the Nature and Causes of the Wealth of Nations.*

## Questions to Consider

1. Have you ever changed your behavior in direct response to a change in economic policy? When and why? Would you react again in the same way if the situation recurred?

2. Are you an optimizer of your future income? What are your biggest concerns with respect to national economic policy?

# Economic Growth and Human Behavior
## Lecture 3—Transcript

Welcome back. In the first 2 lectures of this course, we've examined what works and why it's worked in all of the economies of the world with regard to economic growth and with regard to the macro economy. What we've discovered has been a bit of a mess. We've determined what makes an economy successful and which ones we think are the most successful, but in that process, what we've discovered is that they're very different. What we would expect to find, some similarities, some stream of common ideals, some stream of common policies and activities, really isn't apparent. We found an awful mess of very different economies at very different stages of growth, many of which were successful.

We've also found, on the opposite end, lots of economies that were unsuccessful and also had widely varying very different policies. In some sense, what we can immediately discover is that thinking in terms of economic policies or even economic schools of thought and isms isn't all that helpful. It doesn't really help us understand the difference between the successful economies and the unsuccessful economies. For that reason we might begin to first ask what use is it to have these different schools of thought. I'm not saying that they're not useful, but what I will say is that in some sense this is a mistake. It's a mistake to try to tie these economic schools of thought and these policy choices to successes or failures.

In fact, what we should be doing is to not really expand those definitions or look for a new school of thought, but to really change the question. The real question, the question we should always be asking, is what exactly makes people change their behavior? What makes them change their behavior in ways that leads to economic growth? In that sense, what we need to do is change this level of analysis from headline ideologies, big policies, schools of thought, and think about individuals, think about human beings. The individual needs to be the level of analysis. That's what matters. It's to that subject that we turn our attention now.

If you remember nothing else about economics and nothing else about this course, remember this: People respond to incentives. People respond to incentives, and that's what makes economic behavior change and that ultimately is what leads to the differences between successes and failures. But, if you have room for a little bit more, let's expand that one nugget and add this: People don't always respond the way you think they will, and that's a big problem for economics. People do respond to incentives, but often very differently and not always the way that you think that they will.

Behind the isms and the ideology of the free market is really just another story of incentives. In fact, when I think about the free market, that's what I think about. I think about this story of incentives. Here's my story of incentives that relates to the entirety of the free market. If someone asks me in a cab or over lunch in 30 seconds, one minute or less, tell me about the free market, I'd say the free market is really a story of incentives, and the story is really very simple. In free markets, you reap all the benefits of your actions, and you also incur all the costs of your actions. That's about all there is to it. That's what makes them free; that's what makes them work. The reaping of the benefits and the incurring of the costs are exactly the incentive structure we face, and that's the magic behind free markets. That's what makes most people love them and sometimes hate them.

Free markets really take our natural self-interested behavior and, the idea is, channel our greed toward something that is productive and socially beneficial. I'm greedy. I want a lot of money. I want to have more for myself. So what do I have to do? I have to give you something that you want, something that you'll choose and that you'll pay for. I have to build a better mousetrap for you, offer a better service, more value for the cost. That's a good incentive story. I'm going to reap the benefits and I'm going to incur the costs of any failure. That's because in free markets set failure can be really disastrous. Free markets really don't go along with the idea of a safety net at all. In free and open markets there is no safety net, and that means all the more incentive to be very productive. In fact, we could say that in free markets you have the strongest incentives to be really productive. In fact, we could say we have great inequality because in some sense the flipside of strong incentives are big inequalities. If without the inequalities, what would be the incentive? It does sound great, but that story of free markets, as simple as it is, as powerful as it is, and as successful and true as it has been in many cases, it actually presumes an awful lot, a lot that's hidden or at least not often discussed in those one and a half or 2 minute discussions of why we like free markets.

A couple of things have to be true for free markets and that simple incentive story to work, and these things are the things that really get in the way. It's that human behavior that goes awry sometimes. Here's just a flavor for that. For free markets to work, for that system of incentives to be really successful, this has to be true: Productive behavior, that is economically productive behavior, has to be more profitable than the alternatives. What are the alternatives you might ask? There's fraud, theft, corruption. There are all sorts of socially unproductive behavior, all sorts of ways to get rich, to make money, and to live well without actually building better mousetraps, providing better services. For free markets to work, that has to be true, but we know that that's not always true.

Another thing that has to be true and that often gets in the way when humans get involved in translating incentives into action is the story of risk and a tolerance for risk. In free markets we love the story of the successful entrepreneur who risks it all on a crazy idea and ends up being the next Apple or Microsoft or Google. But, the truth of it is you have to have a lot of tolerance for risk to engage in that activity, and that's often not easy. Economic ventures like that take time and risk and, when there's no safety net, there could often be a shortage of people willing to do that. Without a real tolerance for risk in a culture or society where risk tolerance isn't something people are accustomed to or feel is worth the effort, these ventures will never get started. If those ventures never get started, then behavior never becomes productive and that incentive system just sort of breaks up and doesn't work. It's a really big problem and one to which we'll turn our attention in later lectures.

Yet another thing has to be true—and this is just the short list—and that is that trust or confidence must be present. People must have trust or confidence in the rules of the game, and hence in the other players and in their activities. It's not enough that I believe in the rules of the free-market economy and I'm willing to follow them. I need to believe that you believe in them too and that you're going to follow the same rules or at least be constrained by abusing the rules or going a bit wayward. If I'm worried about you being my partner, and I'm worried about you being corrupt or cheating me, then I'm not going to behave in a way that's productive, even if I myself want to do so. That trust or confidence is very hard to manufacture, and we could ask ourselves where it really comes from. Is it a cultural phenomenon? Is it ever-present? Is it something in the economics and in the policies and in the leaders, or does it come from someplace else altogether? Without trust, without confidence in the rules of the game, a free-market story as elegant and as beautiful as it is, and I believe that it is, it can break down. The problem is, even in the most elegant stories, there are lots of ways for things to go wrong.

The biggest reason that there are lots of ways for things to go wrong, even if you seem to get the policies right, even if you seem to get the rules right, is that humans are in charge. If you think about it, all economic behavior, all economic outcomes like a big economy, a rich economy, lots of jobs, they depend on human beings, you and I making choices and changing our behavior. You can change policies all you want at the top. You can change ideas and change the names of schools of thought, but if human beings don't actually change the way they behave, nothing changes. At the end of the day it does have to be that individual story. That's why this focus on individuals is really so important, why it's that missing ingredient that we needed in those first 2 lectures, why we couldn't tell winning from losing, because we weren't looking at the human beings behind those stories. The closer we look, the closer we'll get to our answers.

If we think about it, one of the bigger problems of coordinating economic behavior is getting human beings to trust one another. If we think about it, most economic behavior that's productive isn't just solely individual. It does require coordinated action. Even if it's not exactly planned in advance, they have to be timed in a way so as to go together. Let me explain what I mean. If you think about being a producer, let's say you wanted to have a bakery or you want to build cars or whatever it is you want to do, if you want to produce economic goods and services, you want to sell them to somebody. But, it's really hard to sell them before you make them. Especially for services, you can't sell them really before you make them. It's really difficult. You need to sell them when you deliver them or after the fact. If you can't sell them before you make them, then somebody has to take the risk of making them without knowing if they'll be sold. It's a risky venture and yet there's no easy way to coordinate that. I myself might want to buy your goods, I might want to buy your car, buy your baked goods or your services, but I want to see them first. I'm going to want to see if they're good or not, and you never really know if you could trust me. Maybe I said I'm going to buy it, and then maybe I'll change my mind, and you'll be stuck with a lot of product, a lot of expenditure, and a lot of risk that goes nowhere.

Let's just assume that you get past that problem, and you have enough people that you could trust to get economic behavior going. Where does that lead you? A little bit can lead to a lot in economics. In fact, once you have a little bit of sales, a little bit of success, it tends to beget more and more success. I see you succeeding in your business, and I have more confidence that maybe I can succeed in mine. It's a great thing, but it's also one of the complex things about economics and what makes it work well. Human beings like to see activity, and they emulate what they see. We see others acting in a way that succeeds, and we mimic it or copy it. If we don't see it, we don't copy it. There's this natural momentum: Sales that work beget more sales, and that success leads to more success even if nothing else changes. Even if the policies don't change or even if they do change, if you see success, it tends to work and its momentum builds. This expectation of things going right can be a real hard won secret of success for any economy.

In the 1930s, this was a key problem. We had the Great Depression in the United States and in most of the West, and part of what happened if you listen to any of the music or read the literature or see the movies is that people just lost faith. They lost their confidence in the economy and in the leadership and in the idea that things could be better. John Maynard Keynes, a famous economist who thought a lot about the Great Depression, maybe more than anyone else, called these ideas animal spirits. He said somewhere in the ether there's this belief, this feeling we get. There's this sense of I trust this—I'm confident. I want to move forward; I want to take a risk. Or, there's this sense of, I don't know, deep inside, deep in the gut, this isn't going to work. This isn't going to work. We've lost our way. We have entered into a period in which the economy doesn't work anymore. Even if I act in the way I did before, and even if I act aggressively, things aren't going to work out. Those animal spirits do seem to be present with human beings. We don't always know what's behind them or where they come from, but they do matter a lot because at the end of the day when I feel confident, when I act, when I buy, or when I take a risk, it makes the opportunity for us to live in a better economy. If no one does that, we're trapped no matter what the policies do.

This is actually something you might want to think about. Imagine this, and you've always done this and I've always done this, but think about being in an economy coming out of a depression. It's a period of time in which people are really struggling economically, where they've lost their faith, where they have seen their fortunes evaporate, where they have seen their friends go without work, without jobs, maybe without food. These conditions exist today and have always existed in the world. It's difficult, we'd like to get out of them, but what would you do? What would you do if you were that leader? How would you instill confidence in people?

You might think about what policies you'd change, you might think about what it is you would do that would be different, but could you make people more confident? What would you say that would really work? What would you do that would prove to them that now is the time to act, to be aggressive and act aggressively, to take those chances, to believe in each other, and in believing in each other, lifting all of ourselves out of this economic mire. You could be passionate and you could be the world's greatest orator, and that might still be very difficult. Instilling confidence is hard to do. We don't exactly know where it comes from or how we can do it.

One of the problems is something that we understand in economics a bit better now. Thirty or 40 years ago economics wasn't really all that conscious about this level of human behavior, but in fact, it's become more important. In the '70s and '80s 2 famous psychologists, Amos Tversky and Daniel Kahneman, experimented and began to try out economic theories to understand how frames, how the context in which humans understood the stories of economic problems or economic choices, mattered. What they learned is that the frames matter a lot. The context, the bed in which a choice lives, the bed in which a policy is presented, matters as much as the policy itself.

As one small example, we know that humans are more aggressive in response to a loss. They are risk averse. In other words, we hate losing more than we like winning. If you frame an economic policy in terms of what might be lost as opposed to what might be gained, people actually respond differently. They respond more aggressively to that. That's important because it means it's not just the policy, it's not just the school of thought or the ism, it's the people and how they interpret it. It's the frame and it's the message and it's the messenger, and it's the context and the plot and the scenery. Because all those things matter, the story of economic growth is a lot more complex than just choosing the right school of thought.

How do you get people to take risks in a weak environment? It's safer to just do the same things you always have or to hold back, to put the money under the mattress. Or, if you're in a world like we're in today where there can be global flows of capital, to not put your money into the local economy that's poor and struggling and needs help, but to take that money and to put it in someplace safe. Send it to that Swiss bank account; put it in Treasury bonds in the United States. Put it in something that is safe and secure, even if where it's really needed is where you live and where you want to see things happen. This is a problem because it means that in economics, we can enter into a vicious cycle of failure breeding more failure, even if we make all the right moves at a policy level. Of success, breeding more success, even if there are missteps and policies vacillate from here to there or we have some policies that seem to disincentivize productive behavior. No confidence equals no confidence and when people are in charge it's hard to break out of these vicious cycles. If you can't change their behavior, make them think differently and act differently, at the end of the day you'll have no success. That means that breaking out of these cycles is really tough. Beliefs matter. Good economies make that leap; other economies don't.

You could sit back and think maybe it's all about staging and about scenery and about the way that a story is presented or about confidence, whether it makes sense or not, and that's kind of true. We've seen this before. We know that people when they are confident seem to be able to perform better. An athlete that believes that they can jump over that bar or run faster than the competition sometimes can, but it's got to be about more than that. It's a complex mix, but it has to come together in some way. The good economies we've seen in Lectures One and Two, through all the diverse ideologies that they followed, they've made that leap. Through some spark, some combination of things, they make the leap to generate a seed of confidence. That seed of confidence flourishes and nourishes the next generation in the further actions, and stepping out further onto the ledge and taking more risks and ultimately leading to more productive, more successful economic behavior.

Other times that doesn't happen. For example, let's suppose that you live in an economy that's been heavily restricted by government activity, where no one can choose where to work, how to work, what to produce, or what to charge. That's easy to remedy. We've seen a lot of success with free trade and open competition as economic policies. In fact, I would say there has been more success around those policies than any others. But let's suppose that you make that change. You go from being the Soviet Union in 1990 with economic collapse with a state-led approach to announcing shock therapy overnight and opening the world to free trade and open markets, saying go out, open your businesses, build what you want, produce what you want, and sell it at the price that you like. Will anyone care? Will anyone react? Will they, hearing that news, actually act in the way that you think they would? They're free to do so now. They're free to build, sell, produce, market, buy, but will they? They don't have to. I guess that's the main point. They can do whatever they want. They can hear the policy, they can see it written on the walls, they could read it in the law books, and believe that it's going to be followed, but action is one step beyond that. For that, you have to get inside the human mind and understand it a little bit better. What makes policies go from being announcements, beliefs about schools of thought, to actually being followed, acted in the seeds of further productive behavior?

You could actually have a problem in which people hear a policy like free and open markets and the ability to price and produce and sell what they want when they want to whom they want. And bearing the risks and accepting the costs of actions and doing well, you could actually have them go in the opposite direction or start to cheat the system. It's really hard to make people always bear the cost of all their actions. In some ways, that's a key snag in all economic ideology based on free markets. It's a good approach, but it's not the only approach. That's why economies like the United States and Western European economies that have free-market approaches need to have strong adherence to the rule of law, need to have some ability to constrain bad behavior and punish those who go astray and not act fairly. If they don't bear the costs of their actions, individuals taking advantage of free markets will deter even others from playing fairly. If the rules aren't enforced, it's hard to encourage good behavior. After all, people respond to incentives. If one of the incentives is cheat and you won't get caught, cheat and you'll get away with it, then you'll encourage more cheating.

I saw one of the most spectacular examples of this in some of my travels. I went to a high-flying, very successful developing economy in Asia. In the paper was this story of this upstart entrepreneur, a real rags-to-riches person, had nothing growing up and had grown into owning and operating the most successful tire business in the largest city in this economy. The tire business was important because as the economy grew more people could afford motorcycles, mopeds, and even cars and buses. This was the story of a very successful entrepreneur who took the risks when rules were changed, who reacted to the free market in the way one would hope by taking a risk and building things, but then the story went on. It was discovered that in fact the great sales and the great success that had been experienced had a common story. It seems that most of the people driving into have their tires changed had run over nails, and it turns out that they'd run over a very similar type of nail. After further investigation it was discovered that the secret to the success of this fabulous tire manufacturer and seller in this developing economy was that at night he went around all the busy intersections and threw boxes of nails out. Then, when they brought the tires in to be replaced and patched, he'd pull the nails back, put them in a box, and go make his rounds the next night. That's not productive behavior, but it's economically profitable behavior. Unless there's a way to constrain that, you can multiply that 10, 20, 100-fold and see how all these activities could fold in on each other, how seeing some success would encourage people not to act productively and to treat each other fairly, but to do the opposite and to sow the seeds of economic destruction.

A big problem behind economic policies and when they work and when they don't, particularly when humans are involved, is actually really simple. It's the problem that's as simple as, well, it's almost tautological. Humans are human. Humans are human, which means that they don't always act in the same way. People don't always do things that are predictable. They're not always logical or rational. They're also not likely to believe you just when you say something. They're at least skeptical. I like to say that people are like the state of Missouri. If you don't know, the state of Missouri's motto is "Show Me," and most people are like that. They want to see something before they believe it. If they have to see it before they believe it, it's really hard to show them if you have no success to start from, which is another reason why success tends to beget success and failure tends to beget failure. The macroeconomic complexity doesn't take these root connections. It doesn't take the fact that these root connections must be true and they must be obvious; they must be apparent and present in an economy.

At the end of the day, what we can take away from understanding human behavior is a bit straightforward, but here it is. Policies aren't enough. You can copy the economic policies of the leading economies of the world, pick any one of them or pick the ones that seem to be the most true. Were I to choose, I would probably try to emulate most of the economic policies of the Western economic powers at the end of the 19th and early 20th century. I'd emulate the United States, which is not too different from a lot of the other policies that have been successful. But, even if you wrote those policies down, even if you wrote them into law, carved them in granite, convinced everyone that you had in fact agreed to change economic policies, they'd have to believe them to work. Policies that aren't believed don't work, so even the same policies can fail in different circumstances. I think that's part of the reason that we see economic success and economic failure in a broad spectrum of economic stories. We see very state-led approaches that succeed and very free-market approaches that succeed, and state-led approaches that fail and free-market approaches that fail. The reason isn't so much the policy always as it is, that if no one believes them, if there's not that confidence, it's difficult. The recipe's a little more complicated than just having the right ingredients.

The second thing that goes along with this is that confidence matters an awful lot and confidence is, kind of like Keynes's animal spirits, a bit in the ether. We don't always know where it comes from or how we keep it, but when we've got it, it's good. If you don't have it, you need it to make it work. In fact, confidence is so valuable that confidence even in a bad policy can be better than no confidence in a great policy. It sounds paradoxical, but it's true. If someone believes that a policy's going to work or that things have changed, even if it's poorly constructed or even if the incentives don't align in a way that really should lead to really productive behavior, it could have some success. Sometimes economies in which people place a lot of faith and have a lot of confidence work better than economies that have better rules, try harder, work harder. It's just the way that that goes. Confidence matters all that much. For that reason, we often see that success breeds success—sometimes even too much. Success can be so driven by momentum that people can begin to take it for granted and not really scrutinize the source of the success. You can believe so much in the fact that you'll win that you never question what it is that leads to your winning to begin with. That's the problem that seems to lie behind economic bubbles and bursts and recessions and depressions, and it's a question to which we'll return. It's a question that lies beyond this element of policy and rests squarely in the realm of human behavior, in what makes people respond in the way that they do.

Another policy would be that fundamentals take place at the personal level. When I speak about fundamentals, what I mean is the fundamental sources of economic stability and growth are really ones that we can see at the individual level. We can see success in free-market economies because people begin to act productively, and they take it for granted that they should act productively. They instill in their children and the people around them this idea of acting productively and adhering to the rules of the game. These fundamentals are really rooted not so much in written laws, although they are there to a degree, as much as they are in the ideology of the individual, in the beliefs of the individual toward the economy.

Another point that goes right along with that would be that it's the framing of the policies as much as the policies. The framing of the policies in time, in culture, and in place is paramount. You could take the same leader and put them in a different economy, put them in a different culture, and in a different economic circumstance, and they'd fail. If you'd put them in the right economic circumstance in the right culture at the right time, they'll succeed. This is what makes it so different. This is why cheating off your neighbor or copying policies, even copying words and frames, doesn't often work. There have to be recipes that are really individualized to economies. Framing is important because human beings need frames, and we think about frames. This is why such seemingly different or controversial policies work and why the same policy doesn't work everywhere. This was the big conundrum leading out of our first 2 lectures and it's one of the first conundrums that any economic historian faces. What's the root of success? What's the root of failure? I see the similarities; I see differences. I see fewer patterns that I would like, and yet I need to emulate and find the root of that success. It's important. It's one of the most profound questions in all of human existence. How do we enable people to live better lives year in and year out? How do we make them economically secure, individually and personally secure? How do we lead to a more peaceful world where people aren't battling over resources, frightened to death that they won't have enough for tomorrow or feeling threatened by the economic successes of their neighbors and of sister economies and sister countries?

To get at that question, to get at that answer, means moving much beyond schools of thought, means moving far beyond these simpler stories of economic policy and getting to the individual level and asking, if that policy works why did it work with that person at that point in time? What was it that motivated them to change their behavior? Was it the written rule? Was it the context and the timing? Was it its combination with so many other policies and historical events? This is what makes understanding macroeconomic growth so difficult, so challenging, and to some degree so enriching, why we can bring to bear all sorts of difference forces and ideas to understand what makes human beings who we are—beautiful, complicated, difficult, and often difficult to manage in a way that's productive and that leads to better livelihoods.

In closing, you might think of it this way. When we think about economic policies, we're really talking about the plan, and a plan is a good thing. Plans are important. Plans guide our behavior, and we need plans to bring together our activities in a way that makes us productive and makes us effective. But in order for a plan to work, a plan has to be followed. A plan will be followed in some circumstances but not in others, and that's what makes economic policymaking and strategizing for growth and leading for growth so difficult. That's what makes it the job of that politician, of that leader, that president, that prime minister, to look forward, pull forth the words, and cast the story that instills confidence in people. It's not an ism. It's not an ideology. It's not that that works. It's whatever makes people respond, what makes human beings behave in a productive way. That's the root of economic growth, and that's what we must understand to understand how to make lives better and richer for the future.

# The Birth of the Western Free Market
## Lecture 4

When you and I think about Industrial Revolution, we imagine factories, and we imagine people working in cities. But those people couldn't have worked in the factories and they couldn't have gone to the cities if they didn't have enough food to leave the farm, and it's really what led to this whole process of industrialization.

The idea of a growing economy, a world where successive generations lived better and better, was once as new as the Internet or cell phones. In fact, until approximately 1500, world economic growth was so slow and weak as to be almost imperceptible. Real economic growth didn't get underway until the late 17th and early 18th centuries, when advances in agricultural productivity in Great Britain and Western Europe gave people some security from the threat of famine.

Before the Industrial Revolution, the work of almost 90 percent of the population was in some way related to agriculture. Scientific advances, such as the idea of crop rotation, led to increased productivity that brought with it such benefits as excess labor—a pool of workers who were no longer needed on farms. This excess labor, in turn, was the key to **scale production**; that is, production on a much larger scale than would be possible from an individual craftsman. Without this revolution in agriculture, there would have been no workers to fuel the Industrial Revolution.

The Industrial Revolution represented an overall jump in productivity to about 20 times its usual rate. This revolution was driven, not by one invention or idea, but by an entire socioeconomic system. Such innovations as scale production, mechanization, and specialization played a significant role in this self-reinforcing system.

In England, these changes absolutely transformed life and society, although not always for the better. One of the most fundamental secrets of the Western economic miracle was the idea of open and free markets—markets in which individuals could choose for themselves what to produce and what to charge for it. Adam Smith pointed out that free markets run on the self-interest of the producers; if someone makes the best product, consumers will buy it, and the producer will gain. In other words, the secret to wealth is to eliminate the control of a central power and let individuals choose for themselves; when they do, they will actually be working for the good of society as a whole.

**That's the only organizing principle that free markets run on: responding to the incentives of the market. Producers and consumers coordinate their activity through the price mechanism and through transacting, and nothing else is really needed.**

The economic miracle of the Industrial Revolution is still influential today. It created from relatively average societies the richest economies in the world, and those economies remain rich more than 100 years later. Is this success solely attributable to democracy and the rule of law that arose in Western Europe? As we've seen, the West took one path to success, but there seem to be other paths, as well.

Adam Smith's phrase "the invisible hand" sums up the free-market economy—the idea that competition, open markets, and freedom are consistent with socially responsible and beneficial activity. This is the classical economic story, and for many, it goes hand in hand with democracy. There are numerous examples throughout history, however, of economies that are successful without being democratic. Indeed, we might say that the theories that followed from the Western miracle were, in some sense, blinded by the fact that the results of that miracle were so profound and so important. ■

## Important Term

**scale production**: The ability to produce on a large as opposed to an individual scale; realized with the advent of the Industrial Revolution.

## Suggested Reading

Bastiat, *Economic Fallacies*.

Bhagwati, *In Defense of Globalization*.

De Soto, *The Mystery of Capital: Why Capitalism Triumphs in the West and Fails Everywhere Else*.

Diamond, *Guns, Germs and Steel: The Fates of Human Societies*.

Keynes, *The Economic Consequences of the Peace*.

Landes, *Revolution in Time: Clocks and the Making of the Modern World*.

Smith, *An Inquiry into the Nature and Causes of the Wealth of Nations*.

## Questions to Consider

1. Have you ever changed your behavior in direct response to a change in economic policy? When and why? Would you react again in the same way if the situation recurred?

2. Are you an optimizer of your future income? What are your biggest concerns with respect to national economic policy?

# The Birth of the Western Free Market
## Lecture 4—Transcript

Welcome back. In the last lecture, we discussed the roots of human economic behavior and how those economic behaviors relate to policies for growth. We even discussed a little bit about how sometimes those fundamentally important human economic behaviors hide behind schools of thought, labels, and isms. In this lecture, we're going to talk about the whole invention of modern economic growth and the fact that modern economic growth was invented in the West, in Western Europe, in places like England and France and Germany, and it migrated quickly to the USA. This lecture is all about that birth, that first miracle, the Western economic miracle of growth.

One of the more difficult things to really get your hands around when you think about a profound sociological and human change is how much it renders the past almost unimaginable. But in order for us to really understand our present and to plan for our future, we must appreciate the past. Believe it or not, at one time the idea of a growing economy, a world where successive generations actually lived better and better, when we looked forward to a better lifestyle for ourselves and for our children as we aged, that was once as new as the Internet and Google and cell phones. Believe it or not, things like that, huge technological changes like e-mailing and web browsing, they're really only a few years old and they sweep the nation. They take over our lives and fundamentally change the way that we live, just like electricity and telephones did in generations that preceded.

Believe it or not, a world in which the Internet didn't exist isn't so far into the past and yet it's almost impossible to imagine a world like that. Would kids today really be able to understand a world without Google, a world without the Internet, a world without computers everywhere they looked, on their phones, everywhere? It's difficult, but believe it or not, at one point the simple idea that the macro economy itself would grow, that the overall economic pie would get larger, and there was a world lying ahead of us where everyone, not just a few individuals, but where everyone could live a little bit better—an idea of a world where one's wealth and their well being wasn't just a transfer from one to another, not just a giant poker game where my winnings or your losses, but was more of a natural state of affairs—that was a huge mind shift, something that the world and the economies of the West had to confront at the beginnings of their great transformation just a few hundred years ago.

Can you actually imagine that? Can you imagine a world where the idea of growth was fundamentally new? We're not talking about a lost decade where no one expected the economy to grow. We're not talking about a few years that weren't good, but the complete absence of the idea that the world of economic living was about growth, that every year would be better than the last. Believe it or not, that was the state of the world economy up until about the middle of the 18$^{th}$ century, when in the West, and in England in particular, the Western world really invented this idea of modern economic growth. Prior to that point, as hard as it is to imagine, no one really thought of themselves, no one really thought of the economy, no one thought of a world in those terms before. It was an entirely new idea.

We could tell the story. We could say once upon a time, boys and girls, there was no growth in the world. In fact if we didn't just tell the story, but looked at the good data that we have, we'd say that to the best of anyone's knowledge, economic living standards across the world grew almost not at all from the year one let's say until about the year 1000, our best estimates—and they're a bit crude but pretty good estimates—tell us that the economy's of the world grew at only about one-tenth of 1% per year. That's positively lousy. It's so slow and so weak that you wouldn't even know it if you were living in a world like that. You wouldn't perceive growth at that rate. It wouldn't seem like growth at all. It would seem like static or noise, a few years of good, a few years of bad, but really year after year almost nothing changed. If you wanted to really think about it in sort of standard statistical terms, you might think about a world in which you earned $1,000 a year and, maybe if you were lucky, 10 years later you'd have an extra $72 in your pocket. Or, if you're earning a dollar an hour in one year, then 10 years you're going to earn all of $1.07 an hour. Such a small change really doesn't fundamentally change the way we live, and it didn't change the way that people thought about themselves and their lives.

It really seems safe for us to presume that for a millennia, or maybe even a millennia and a half, until at least the year 1,500, maybe even beyond that, sons lived just about as well as their fathers did and expected to. Daughters expected a family life much like their mother's life, and no one had really any reason to think about a better life for their children. Maybe they hoped for it; maybe they believed that through luck or villainy or chance they'd live better. But, the idea that through their own efforts they could live better and so could anyone else's children—that was just a completely new idea.

In a context like that, in a world where there is no economic growth, all riches, all wealth is made by only a few ways, and none of them are all that good. There's domination. You could sort of dominate, take power, and seize wealth. You could be a villain and take it on a small scale or run across it, or maybe you'll get lucky and stumble upon it. Maybe you can dig it out of the ground somewhere. But, the ideas that we have today are so different from that. We think about ingenuity, talent, working harder, living better, investing in yourself, and taking chances, and of these being the stepping stones on the path to growth. That's really a much more new idea than we might think.

None of this ever got off the ground, none of it really changed markedly anywhere until really about the late 17$^{th}$ century. In the beginning of the 17$^{th}$ century, there were already scientific discoveries and some evidence of the world picking up its pace of economic growth, but it really wasn't measurable. It wasn't appreciable, and it didn't reach the level that we would associate with modern economic (and what we might think of as relatively rapid) growth until about the late-17$^{th}$ and early-18$^{th}$ century when, in particular, advances in agricultural productivity in Great Britain and in Western Europe led the way. These discoveries, these novel changes, generated a safe distance from famine, from the threat of disease, of food insecurity, and those things that kept people on the brink of poverty.

Let's talk about it this way. It's a very big story, but let me give you a short rendition about how the West went from a sort of poor economy of the Middle Ages—and I'm sure you can feel that imagery and think about people living in very humble circumstances with very little to their name—how it went from that to the hotbed of economic growth. Here's the short story. To be honest, it's a little bit different than most people might think because we associate this with the Industrial Revolution, with the rise of machines and scale production, and that's in part true, but there's a missing element.

The missing element that's all-important is the first thing that happened. The first thing that happened was that there was an agricultural revolution. If you think about it, that sort of makes sense, but maybe it refreshes your memory a bit and it helps to go back and think about what life would have been like in a world prior to the Industrial Revolution. In the world prior to the Industrial Revolution, almost everybody was a farmer. Almost 90% of the population in fact was in some way related to agriculture. It wasn't that they all loved agriculture, although there were many good things about it, that's just how many people it took to provide the food and the food resources needed to sustain society. You really had to dedicate that many people.

can think about it in a different way. Farming was really relatively unproductive. It was so unproductive that almost everybody had to do it just to keep the population alive, just to keep people fed. This revolution really started with some scientific advances, and the scientific advances were all-important. Some of them were really simple, but there were scientific advances about crop rotation, about how to move from one crop in one season to a different crop that was not subject to the same pests as the previous crop, how to infuse nitrates into the soil and irrigate in ways that were better, much better than had been introduced in the previous millennia. Suddenly there was this advance of productivity. With that advance of productivity came all manner of benefits that would transform the world.

For the first time, because you have an agricultural revolution, because you had more food being produced, and because society could generate enough food to be more secure, you actually had for the first time ever what we might call excess labor. When I say excess labor I don't mean unwanted labor, I just mean there were people who no longer needed to work on farms. There was enough productivity that about 2/3 or 80% of the proportion of people who worked on farms were needed to produce the same amount of goods and services, to produce the same amount of agricultural output. You could reduce the number of farmers and still have an economy that could feed itself, so where did these new people go? That's part of the story.

These magic formulas in farming, the crop rotation and others, we might say that they released workers, they released young men and sometimes young women to other uses, to specializations in the work that previously they couldn't dream of or they couldn't afford to do. This excess labor was really the key to something that was vital to the Industrial Revolution, and that's what we call scale production. Scale production is producing not on a small scale, on a craftsman's scale, an individual scale, but on a massive scale, on the factory scale, something we're intimately familiar with today.

Without that agricultural revolution, there would've been really no one to staff or to supply the workers for the Industrial Revolution that followed. When you and I think about Industrial Revolution, we imagine factories, and we imagine people working in cities. But, those people couldn't have worked in the factories and they couldn't have gone to the cities if they didn't have enough food to leave the farm, and it's really what led to this whole process of industrialization. The people that staffed the Industrial Revolution were the farmers. They were the ones that went from being beholden to the farm to being available to work in cities and to work in the factories. That was the magic that first led to large-scale productivity growth and the birth of modern economic growth in England.

It's a big jump. It was a huge change. The ability to take workers and release them into cities, to release them into uses that previously no one could staff, was enormous. In fact, the Industrial Revolution represented what we might think of as a jump in overall productivity to about 20 times its usual rate—20 times, that's extraordinary. Try to imagine that today, your own productivity rising by 20 times. It sounds great, but it's almost unimaginable, one person equating to 20 over a short period of time. Yet that's how fundamental the change was. It's easy to see how that would change your view of society, how it would change your own personal reality.

But, it wasn't a silver bullet sort of solution. The Industrial Revolution wasn't about one technology or one invention or one idea; it was really driven by an entire socioeconomic system. It wasn't just that one individual had an idea or that there was a new law passed or a new invention, it's that the whole of society fit cleanly with this new idea of self-interested motivations, of productivity in investing in oneself in producing what one wanted when one wanted to produce it. It was driven by things like scale production. In fact I'd say that scale production is the overall key to the productivity growth that is the hallmark of the Industrial Revolution. What really made society wealthier was that it was more productive, a given amount of resources could produce more goods and services than before. That's what productivity is. That's what it means to grow more productive over time and to become more efficient.

This idea, this description of scale production, and the increase in productivity that followed or went along with it was probably best described by Adam Smith in his hallmark fantastic book *The Wealth of Nations*. Written in 1776—a year that I always remember well of course—*The Wealth of Nations* really described how the Industrial Revolution was changing England and shaping the world to come. It was also the seabed to more economic ideas than any other single book in human history. Those ideas are still fundamental today, and it's something we'll look at shortly.

At the same time that people were engaging in the trends from the farm to the city, they were also engaged in mechanizing processes that previously had only been done by hand, and this also went hand and glove with scale production. Previously, all work was done by humans or with modest tools. But, if you have scale production, suddenly you can think in larger scenes. You can think about larger scale and really drive production through mechanization and, through that, you can add value.

As I said before, it wasn't an invention, but a self-reinforcing system that really led to this magic growth in productivity. It led to this virtuous cycle where ingenuity was rewarded. We talked about this in a previous lecture. The incentive to be ingenious, to invest in oneself and to come up with an idea, got much sharper all of a sudden because the rewards of being ingenious, the rewards of having a new idea or a better mousetrap or a better way to produce things, was suddenly rewarded by a free-market system. That meant that people had the incentive to invest in themselves, in the talents and skills that they wanted to hone, and also in those products and those services they wanted to produce. They could invest in factories. They could invest in larger-scale production, where as previously there would've been no one to consume those things.

Another outcropping of the Industrial Revolution would've changed the way people thought about saving. When we think about saving, one of the primary motivations we have is what we might call precautionary saving. You save for a rainy day. That's been an enduring theme behind saving since saving was invented at the beginning of time. When people save, in part they're saving because something could go wrong. You could hurt yourself, break a leg, there could be a large storm—anything could happen. But, now there was a new reason to save, not just for the bad things, not just to stave off demise when you suddenly had a run of bad luck, but in fact saving for investment and investment in profitable opportunities. The incentives of the free-market system aligned in such a way that they rewarded efforts of people to not consume things, but to save things, to save their money so that they could invest in ways to build better mousetraps, to bring new services to the market, to educate themselves. Suddenly all of these incentives lined up very closely together.

In particular, one of the things we most closely associate with the Industrial Revolution is specialization. Specialization is a key factor in scale production. When we think about specialization, there are lots of things that go along with it, but it's an inherently social activity. In any production process, you could have an individual producer. Think about building furniture. You could have one craftsman doing everything and building all the furniture himself. He could cut the wood, shave the wood, polish the wood, make all the dowels, cut all the boards, glue everything together, and stain it—the whole process. Or, you could operate in scale and have everyone specialize in only one aspect of the production process. They could not be great at everything, not a jack-of-all-trades, but they could be a master of one trade. In that mastery, in that specialization, lay more productivity. That productivity was part and parcel of the magic that led the West from the Dark Ages to the Modern Age.

With less need for farmers and with more leeway to travel to cities where one could specialize and could work in scale production, could work in manufacturing, one could transform the whole of society, and so it happened. In England, these changes absolutely transformed life and society. It didn't always transform life and society for the better; in fact, some things were certainly for the worse. When we think about the beginnings of the Industrial Revolution, when we think about what we might call that ugly adolescence of industrialization, we certainly think about crowded factories. We think about slums in cities, and we think about poverty on a scale that many had never seen face to face before. We think about the abandonment of rural areas. We think about the dissolution of families. We also think about the spread of material wealth. With the good came some of the bad, but these were all part of that same huge transformation.

That transformation really began in the West. That's vitally important because, since it began in the West, since the economic secret to growth on a scale never contemplated before resided in the West, then thinkers and educators and bright people and leaders associated growth with everything with the West. The idea of Western society became shorthand for societies that grow economically and rapidly. In that lay the jump from the path to economic growth is to be just like a Western society and then that meant that everything might be copied. Since the West had the secret, then we should copy the West if we too want to grow.

What was the secret? What were the ideas? Certainly one could look at Western society and contrast them with other societies and ask what's really different? What really was the secret sauce behind the rise of the West and its huge growth in terms of economic performance and its productivity? By 1850, folks in Great Britain were 5 times as rich as their Chinese counterparts, but how? What was it really about? There was no shortage of ideas, but certainly one of the early chroniclers already mentioned, Adam Smith, had a pretty good idea. One of the most fundamental secrets of the Western economic miracle and its growth was the idea of open and free markets. When I say open and free markets what I really mean are markets where individuals choose for themselves what to produce, when to produce, and what to charge for it. It sounds really simple, but it was much more of a novel idea. What they really meant was by freeing the economy, allowing people to do what they wanted when they wanted, we'd all be better off. It sounds a little shaky, but it was something that was really powerful and an idea that held a lot of sway then and holds a lot of sway now.

Adam Smith in fact had a lot of famous ways of saying this, and some of the quotes I know you'll find familiar. I have a few favorites and I want to recount them for you. Here's one of my favorites that really talks about and encapsulates this idea of free markets and why they work. Smith writes this when he talks about how things get produced in a free-market society and what's good about it. He writes: "It is not from the benevolence of the butcher, the brewer, or the baker that we expect our dinner, but from their regard to their own self interest. We address ourselves not to their humanity, but to their self-love and never talk to them of our necessities but of their advantages."

What's he really saying? He's saying when we think about what we want from society, what we want to have produced, we don't have to ask people to do it out of the goodness of their heart. We just talk about what's good for them. If they make the best beer, if they cut the best meat, if they brew the best of anything, then we'll buy it and they will gain. That's the only organizing principle that free markets run on, responding to the incentives of the market. Producers and consumers coordinate their activity through the price mechanism and through transacting, and nothing else is really needed.

That's a pretty special thing to say. It also gives producers and average people a lot of leeway. Rather than have these choices reside somewhere centrally, like in a powerful source in the parliament or with a king or a monarch, Adam Smith is saying the secret to wealth is to get rid of all that control and to let individuals choose for themselves, even if it means choosing things that on the face of them seem like they might be bad for society. Here's one that always seems bad, buying things from foreign producers instead of domestic producers. Even at that early time Smith said we shouldn't worry about that at all. All we need to do is let these choices—where to buy, how much to buy, and who to buy from—leave these choices up to the producers themselves.

I have another quote that he writes when he talks about preferring domestic producers over foreign, or in this case producing foreign producers over domestic ones. Smith is talking about this magic process, this process by which even those choices which seem like they could harm society actually help it. Listen to this—Smith writes: "By preferring the support of domestic to that of foreign industry, he," meaning a producer, "intends only his own security. And by directing that industry in such a manner as to produce it maybe of the greatest value, he intends only his own gain." Here's the good part: "And he is, in this, as in many other cases, led by an invisible hand to promote an end that was no part of his intention, knows that always the worst for society that it was not part of it." This is the part I think I even like the best. Smith writes: "By pursuing his own interest he frequently promotes that of society more effectually than when he really intends to promote it."

You have to think about that a minute because, in that statement, in that phrasing, in that idea, he's really saying let people make their own choices. When they do, they're actually working for the whole of society. It's not exactly akin to what we think of today. It's not exactly the greed is good story, but it is saying a producer, a merchant, a factory owner, by minimizing their own cost, making choices to buy from abroad, to buy domestically, by minimizing their own cost and making themselves better off, they actually make us better off, sometimes even more so than they do when they want to be charitable. They promote the interests of society more effectually than when they really intend to promote it.

That's the magic of competition. That's part of the story that Smith's talking about. Let producers compete in an open marketplace. If they're forced to compete, the fittest will survive—the leanest, those with the best products, the most value for the money. This idea, this process that to most of us will sound Darwinian, actually comes much earlier. In fact, Darwin borrowed from Smith, not the other way around. The idea of competition and free markets and free choice implies a lot of things that we associate very closely with the Industrial Revolution and the West, things like minimal government involvement. There's nothing in Smith's story about competition and survival of the fittest that really requires a lot of government involvement. This is a private revolution.

There's also the idea of being really open to trade and free trade, trade across borders. Why would that be true? How is that consistent? Think of it this way. If I'm a merchant and when I pursue my own interest I make the whole of society better, then why should you limit my choices? The only thing you could do was rule out things that could make me better off and since our interests are so closely tied you should never limit my choices, so be open to trade across borders, across lands. Any way you slice it, openness to trading and free-market competition go hand in hand. We also think about risk taking, about the idea of private enterprise being central to a good life and a good productive economic environment. We think about entrepreneurship and all the ideas of entrepreneurs taking on new ideas and new risk and creating newer and better products. Those are all fundamental ideas to the West.

It's interesting because when we think about the West and we think about its economic successes, we tend to think about the miracle having occurred a couple of hundred years ago. In fact, that miracle was so influential that it still holds a lot of sway today. The economic miracle that began in the West created from relatively average societies the richest economies in the world. By the beginning of the 20th century, almost all of the wealthy countries in the world were from the West or very close offshoots. They were countries like England, France, and Germany. They were countries like the offshoots, the United States, New Zealand, Austria, and a few others. But, they were rich then. What's perhaps even more amazing is that they're also the rich countries now. If we think about the richest economies in the world today, maybe one thing that's a bit sobering or surprising is that the ones that are rich today were already the richest 100 years ago. That's how profound that early start, that early revolution, meant to the West. It was the beginning of the economic miracle, and it's a miracle whose power has been sustained throughout a century.

In fact, when we think about high-income societies and when we think about modern economies, we're almost always thinking about the West. They're really almost synonymous, almost one and the same. Almost until the last 3 decades have we seen nothing but success in the West and moderate to limited successes everywhere else. The problem is, whether or not it was truly a characteristic of the West, whether or not that growth, that magic formula was really about those societies and those cultures. Was it about democracy and the rule of law and the particular cultures that arose in Western Europe or was it something else? Are all those trappings merely hiding the real secrets to economic growth, or were they so fundamental that the only path to growth seems to be copying them? In fact, we've already alluded to the answer to that and part of the answer is what the West did worked, but there seemed to be more than one path, and there seems to be more than the path that the economies of the West trod 200 years ago.

That was the most influential event in all of economic history I'd say, the Western economic miracle, so influential I would say that virtually everywhere you go, as much as it may seem abrasive to some or not exactly a perfect fit, almost everyone believes in some ways in Smith's invisible hand. That 2-word phrase, the invisible hand, is the representative of the free-market economy. The idea that these ideas of competition, of open markets and freedom, are really perfectly consistent with socially responsible and beneficial activity—the idea that all a government need do to be wealthy and to have an economy that's wealthy is let go and let people choose for themselves.

Let them pursue their own interests narrowly, and that's actually good for the world. It's shorthand for the idea of a marketplace that is self-correcting. When I say self-correcting what I mean is when there's a shortage, eventually the free market fills the shortage. When there's a surplus, eventually the free market gets rid of the surplus. The free market automatically equates supply and demand. When there's a shortage, prices rise and supply equals demand. When there's a surplus, prices eventually fall and supply equals demand again. No one need intervene. It's a very elegant decentralized story, and it's what we call the classical economic story, the idea of a self-correcting free-market economy where prices move. Even if you don't believe in all of it, almost everyone you know has a lot of classical thinking in their minds. We're all classicists, if you will.

We sometimes like to add to that classical idea the idea of a West that's bounded by democracy and other ideas, and surely these are important. In subsequent lectures, we want to talk about the institutions of the West and how they fit into the economic story. But, we could ask already, is democracy vital? Must an economy also have democracy to be economically successful? It may seem so. If the West is the secret and the West is democratic, one might think that's true, but already we can say that it certainly doesn't seem to be a necessary condition. There are plenty of examples throughout history of economies that are successful without exactly being democratic, and economies that perform at similar levels or even better than some of the early winners in the West and yet have very different cultures and very different rules by which they follow. Even the celebrated Protestant work ethic doesn't seem to be a necessary condition, but maybe it has some magic left in it. Maybe there's something important there.

Whenever we think about the Western miracle and what it really means, it's hard to get away from the idea that the West earned it, that it was just a superior society organized in a more fluid way, organized in a better way for economic growth and productivity, that ideas like democracy, freedom of expression, an investment in scientific inquiry, experimentation, boundaries of law, well-guarded, well-established enforced laws were so secret and so wonderful that only the West had them and it had them first. When we think about the failures to have economic growth outside the West, we often attribute those failures to cultural failures.

It isn't that they chose the wrong policy; it's that they're simply not good enough. They simply haven't learned enough about the rule of law and about democracy to really have earned that growth. But, is it so? After all, when we think about the West, it really stumbled upon the idea of growth. There was no monarch or politician with a 5-year plan to grow the economy from 0% per year to something more. It just sort of emerged. It just sort of happened. We have to always ask ourselves the question what's the real reason the West grew? What can we really take away? What are the secrets that were there?

The Western legacy is the most important. It's the burst of growth and the birth of know-how about that growth and its transformation of the whole world, but it's also led to some challenge, maybe even flawed thinking about what are really the secrets to growth. We might say in closing that the theories that followed from the Western miracle were in some sense blinded by the wonderful nature of that miracle, by the fact that it was so profound and so important that we attributed everything in the West to growth and everything about growth to the West and didn't leave our minds open to alternative paths and other explanations. In the ensuing decades and the ensuing centuries, we learned a lot about the Western economic miracle.

We've learned a lot about what made it work. We've learned a lot about productivity growth and how to emulate some aspects of the West without adopting full-scale all the cultural characteristics. Mercifully, we've unlearned some of the things that were untrue. What we continue to learn about the West feeds our thinking about what it will take to render a world richer, more peaceful, and more munificent than ever before. We look forward to that discussion in subsequent lectures and we can take these ideas with us wherever we go because, throughout all of economic history, there's never been a story as good as the Western economic miracle.

# American Economic Strategies
## Lecture 5

> [Our recovery now is] going to come down to our behavior and whether we'll see hope and confidence and reasons to stimulate and act aggressively again. It's going to come down to the confidence of the people and the ideas that they have about their own economy and whether they have faith in it.

The United States has been the largest economy in the world since about 1870, and its story is deeply rooted in classical economic ideas. The classical economic structure is one in which the wealth of a nation rests not in the king's treasury or the amount of oil beneath the soil but in the economic prowess and possibilities of the nation's people.

The good side of classical economics in the United States is that its ideas are closely related to freedom. Pursuing one's dreams and generating wealth are the best things an individual can do for society. However, in a classical economy, one must also take risks and engage in competition, which can result in rewards or losses. Classical economics is also a self-correcting system. If problems occur in the marketplace, classical economics stands back and waits for the system to achieve its own balance.

The story of the economy that gave birth to the American dream began at the end of the Civil War. Since that time, the U.S. economy has flourished, but it has also been severely challenged. In the 1870s, our economy was defined by a complete lack of control, and although it experienced a boom through the early part of the 20th century, it also suffered from a lack of competition and a subsequent loss of public confidence. Around 1913–1914, the government stepped in, creating a central bank, regulations, and a national income tax to promote stability in the financial system.

From 1913 until about 1928, the United States embarked on one of its fastest growth periods. But that period came to an end with the Great Depression, an event that challenged the idea that the economy would self-equilibrate. Unemployment was at 25 percent, but wages weren't falling low enough to bring people back to work. Companies failed, prices collapsed, and the situation kept getting worse. John Maynard Keynes said, "In the long run, we're all dead," meaning that self-correction is worthless if it takes too long. With Keynes came the birth of the idea that a government in this situation should take action to get the economy back on track.

The United States wouldn't be challenged again in the same way until about 2007, with the Sub-Prime Crisis. Oddly, this crisis began because the U.S. economy was so strong and inspired so much confidence that money flowed in easily from around the world and was used sloppily. Most people bought into the idea of the rational investor, that is, that investors know better than anyone else what they need to do to protect themselves. We didn't consider the possibility of irrational behavior and its net effect on the economy. We didn't understand how economic manias take place or how housing booms and asset bubbles emerge.

**[The American dream is] largely an economic dream. It's the embodiment of the rags-to-riches story, of the Horatio Alger story, of entrepreneurs that go into their parents' basement, and with $25 and duct tape, come up with the next great thing.**

When the global capital flows began to shake, when the bubble began to burst, and when it became obvious that the extraordinary rise in housing prices could not be sustained, the United States engaged in the most massive government stimulus and break from self-correction in economic history. We've made a huge bet, and if we're right, we'll have avoided a second Great Depression, but if we're wrong, the United States will no longer be the leading economic light of the world. ■

## Suggested Reading

Faulkner and Shell, eds., *America at Risk*.
Friedman and Schwartz, *A Monetary History of the United States*.
Friedman, *The World Is Flat*.
Keynes, *The General Theory of Employment, Interest and Money*.
Krugman, *The Return of Depression Economics*.

1. What is the most critical change facing the United States now that huge economies, such as those of China and India, are growing more important to the world economy?

2. How has U.S. leadership of the global economy threatened to undo our nation's ability to grow?

# American Economic Strategies
## Lecture 5—Transcript

Welcome back. In the previous lecture, we looked at the broad story of the Western economic miracle, the most important story in all of economic history. In this lecture, we follow up on that lecture with a discussion of the leading economy of the Western economic miracle. Ironically, it's not a European economy, it's not Great Britain, where the Industrial Revolution truly began—it's the United States. Almost ever since the United States emerged from the Civil War, the United States has been the undisputed free-market leader of the world. It's been the hallmark of the Western economic miracle and the economy that embodied all those ideas more so than any other. It's been the undisputed leader of the world economy for more than a century, and we wonder for how much longer will it hold that lead.

We know that the U.S. has been the largest economy in the world since about 1870. It's not just been the largest in terms of the largest economic pie, but it's really been the richest in terms of having the largest per person income level, the largest slices of pie. In fact, we can date this to about 1905, which is about the time the U.S. became, as far as relatively large economies are concerned, the richest economy in the world. It was the leader and the richest economy in the world at the beginning of the 20th century, just as it was at the end of the 20th century.

Already by about the turn of the 20th century the U.S. economy was twice as large as the United Kingdom's economy, which was the world's second largest economy at the time. The U.S. economy remains that large and today represents about 20–25% of the world economy. It remains so since about the middle of the 1970s when, although the U.S. represented a little bit less than 5% of the world population, it represented 25% of all economic output in the world. That's an extraordinary figure, and it tells you a little bit about the economic importance of the United States to the global economy and about the relative rarity of an economy that size. If one economy with 5% or less of the population can be 25% of the world economy, then it must imply a lot of other economies are large, but relatively small in terms of economic output and wealth.

The U.S. really epitomizes this open free-market economic approach driven by entrepreneurship and the quest for innovation. These things are almost synonymous with the story of the American economy. It's an economy where we reward hard work and we value courage and determination perhaps more so than any other economy. It's a great story, and it's an economic story that's closely intertwined with the overall story of what America means to the world and what the United States means to the history of economic development.

If we think about the United States and we think about the story of the United States, we think about a story that's deeply rooted in classical economic ideas. When I say classical economic ideas, what I really mean are these free-market open-economy ideas. To put it a little more clearly, a classical economic idea is an idea that a productive society which becomes a wealthy society is one that's best organized around a system of individual self-interests. This is back that old Adam Smith idea about the invisible hand and about an individual promoting society's good when they pursue their own wealth and their own well-being. It says go ahead and produce what you want, choose what you want to do, act in your own best interest, and no one needs to govern what you do. There's no need for a grand plan set forth by parliament or the president or any other governing body. Do what you think is best, and that is going to lead the society to riches. We don't need to think about anything else. Properly bounded by the law, an individual's pursuit of their own self-interest is in the best interest of society. That's a classical economic idea.

Put another way, the idea of a classical economic structure is one in which the wealth of nations really rests not in a stack of gold or the king's treasury or in the amount of oil that courses beneath the soil, rather the wealth of a nation is in the economic prowess and in the possibilities of its people. It's a very democratic and individualized idea. In fact, when we think about wealth in a classical sense, we need to think about national income—not the income of an individual, not their paycheck or what they earn in some period, but the sum of all incomes in society. When we think about the sum of all of those incomes that's really the overall size of the economy, that's the wealth of a nation, that's its gross domestic product. When we think about the United States, we think about an income-generating machine. It's not just that its power is in marshal superiority, it's also that it's in economic superiority in the ability to create incomes that are high and rising over time for everyone.

It's also based in this economic idea rooted in the U.S. that classical economics is in part about freedom. In fact, I'd say that classical economics is very freeing. It really says go out and pursue your dreams. You have the secret to growth. It's in your cockeyed ideas. It's in your crazy dreams. Go ahead and pursue them. That's the best thing that you can do for all of society or, at least, in pursuit of your dreams, if you realize your dreams, if you become that next generator of the greatest thing, the next gadget that we all have to have, well then that's good for all of us. That's great for all of us. Being that entrepreneur, being that risk taker is part and parcel of living the American dream.

That's the good side and it's mostly a good side for the entrepreneurial story, but there are other sides too. A classical economy, a classical economic idea, is also one that admits that one must take risks to be rewarded, that one must engage in competition to be rewarded. In any risk-taking venture and in any time you have competition, you don't just have winners. You have those that lose. You produce a lot of losses. A classical economic idea says you the individual are responsible for your own losses. In some sense, you really earn your own losses. It's good for people to be productive, and we reward and celebrate people who are productive and who are successful and who have incomes that are high and match their success, that match their ingenuity, that match their relative position versus the competition that they face. It also says that you might be poor, you might have failed, but if you are, in some sense you deserve what you get. You might deserve your lack of income just as much as Bill Gates or Steve Jobs deserve their billions, and that's just all there is about an economic idea. That's a classical idea. You live with the rewards and you live with the losses.

Likewise, classical economics is a system of self-correction. I've mentioned that before, but let me mention it again. It's an important idea. Self-correction means that some of the problems of an economy are best left to heal themselves. Think of it this way. Suppose you have unemployment, too many people and not enough of them can get jobs. A classical economic idea is don't do anything. The market will correct itself. If you have too many people searching for too few jobs, then what we need is the price mechanism to eventually equate supply and demand. A classical response to unemployment is to let the wage level fall so low that eventually those workers are in demand again. Let the system go, and it will correct itself.

In reverse, maybe you have a deficit. Maybe you have too few of something. That's an easier solution. If there's too few of anything, maybe there's too little gasoline and prices at the gas pump are rising, a classical solution is don't do anything. Let the market solve the problem of a price of gasoline that's too high. People will begin to selectively travel. They'll ration their trips. Entrepreneurs will jump into the fray with more fuel-efficient vehicles and other solutions to solve the problem of high gas prices. Classical economics is about letting the market correct itself, letting the market go, and letting everyone be free to provide the solutions and respond to the problems as they arise. That's classical economics, and it's part and parcel of the idea of being in the United States and in that vibrant self-correcting economy.

In an economy like the United States, we tend to think about the best stories that there are, the best stories of any free-market economy, and in this economy we think about the American dream. Whenever I've said that phrase, I've always wondered if other countries had dreams like that, but we know what we mean when we say the American dream. It's largely an economic dream. It's the embodiment of the rags-to-riches story, of the Horatio Alger story, of entrepreneurs that go into their parents' basement, and with $25 and duct tape come up with the next great thing. It's the idea of taking a gamble and taking a risk, but with your ingenuity and a lot of hard work, ultimately receiving the rewards when you reward society with your new invention, with your new idea, with your better way of doing things. This is the society that rewards middle-class people with huge wealth if they can simply surmount the competition. That's a very classical idea. It's an idea of society rewarding the deserving, rewarding those who take risks and win.

These stories are more than just fanciful tales, and they're more than just propaganda. American history is really replete with stories of rags-to-riches ideas. It's replete with stories of folks who've gone from nothing to ultimately become something huge, wealthy merchants, billionaires to becoming titans of industry. It's the flipside of an economy that can take poverty and get rid of it. It can reduce poverty like no other system that's ever invented, and it's the flipside of an economy that was able to take subsistence farmers in one generation, move them to cities, and create wealthy merchants from them.

The story of the American dream and the story of the American economy that gave birth to the American dream is really one that was born in the late 19th century, really at the end of the Civil War, when finally this historically rich resource-rich country was peaceful and there was lots of opportunity, where an overcrowded Europe could send immigrants and send people who were desperate for new opportunities to a land that would welcome them and give them those opportunities. Since that time and even during that period, the U.S. economy has flourished, but it's also been very severely challenged. In fact, before 1900, there was the great boom of the 1870s when the U.S. really made its mark, but what did the economy look like during that period?

Honestly, the economy of the 1870s looks almost completely different from the economy of the 1970s. In the 1870s, you had a U.S. economy that was defined by a lack of any control. It was, in some sense, the real Wild West of economies. There was really no federal government to speak of, there was certainly no central bank, no federal income tax, no social security, no Medicare, and no welfare. Everyone sort of lived by their own wits. We can look at that boom from 1870 to the early part of the 20th century and ask, was that boom a consequence of an economy that was so free where everyone lived by their own wits and there was no government to get in and create a safety net or enforce rules? There was, in fact, no safety net at all by government. Everything was provided by the family or by broader of society. To many, this is still a secret to that fancy wonderful period where growth really took off in the United States. In fact, there was no meaningful regulation of any kind until at least the 1913–1914 period, when we began to have a central bank, a Federal Reserve, when we began to have an economy with a federal income tax and deeper federal regulation of competition.

At that moment, the U.S. economy really began this profound shift, and it moved from being a very free-market economy almost completely unregulated toward the middle. It embarked upon a path that it continues on to this day toward slightly more government involvement, slightly less freedom. It's interesting to examine what that really means. We can begin by asking, what really changed? If it wasn't broken, why did we fix it? In fact, a lot of people look at that period, the 1870s, and say there was a lot that was broken. In fact, this magical, self-organizing, classical economy had a lot of flaws and a lot of problems that almost led the economy to its own downfall.

Among those problems were the pains of self-correction. We talked a bit earlier about how a classic economy self-corrects. When there's a surplus, prices fall; when there's excess demand, prices rise. That sounds good, but the pain of self-correction was often too much for the market to bear. In fact, it was the lack of self-regulation that led to a lot of these self-correction problems. Think of it this way: There were a lot of injustices in the 1870s. When we think about robber barons, when we think about trusts and monopolies really getting a stranglehold on an economy, we think of that period. That's because if you think about it, there was no hint at all of the problems of law enforcement in that period, therefore masters of the universe, robber barons, titans of industry could sort of run amok. They didn't have to be competitive if they didn't want to be. The system needs competition to work.

Any free-market system lives off of competition, but in fact, a free-market system also rewards monopoly. Inherent in a free-market system is an incentive that says while competition is good for the broad society, Adam Smith's invisible hand works because competition forces me to compete, forces me to be better and lower cost relative to my competitors. As a producer, as a titan of industry, as a merchant, the last thing I want is competition. I want less competition, and in fact that's what firms quickly realized. In that great period of growth, lots of firms consolidated and moved together to become monopolies. In that sense, they really handcuffed the invisible hand. Monopolies thwart competition; they eliminated competition. In that sense, this magical idea that pursuing one's self-interest could lead to the public interest was broken.

The punch line to all this is that during this period when lots of abuses of the system were there, and when, in particular, the value of competition was lost because it couldn't be kept strong because monopolies arose and trusts arose, the U.S. had to adapt. We had to find ways to abruptly adapt to these market failures or else risk losing the confidence of the people in the system. People who live and work in an economy that's growing, where there is competitive behavior and people are always trying to provide better services at lower costs, have a lot of confidence. They buy into the system and they support it politically. But, in the reverse situation, when you have monopolies, people being exploited, people seeing that this is not a productive economy, but a giant poker game and we're losing, they abandon the system, and that's the situation the U.S. economy faced.

The government stepped in. It created a central bank to promote some stability in the financial system. It promoted bank regulations that certainly limited the actions of banks but also provided a bit more security about the value of monies put into banks. It generated more trust in an economy that was too Wild West to really hold that trust. To fund some of these interventions, it also implemented at the time a relatively modest, but still controversial, national income tax. We'd busted trusts, broke up monopolies, and fought all manner of anticompetitive behavior. The U.S. economy really stepped away from a purely classical idea that the economy could be completely free and stepped in to try to eliminate flaws in the system, to promote a rule of law that was truly consistent with a competitive free-market idea but that was perhaps underappreciated at the beginning of that period in the U.S. economy. On the spectrum from free markets to fully-state run economies, we begin inching a bit toward the middle. By the middle of the 1913–1915 period, we were taking a very large step.

Most everything stayed more or less the same in the U.S. economy of the early 20th century. It was a really terrifically successful period. From 1913 until about 1928, the U.S. embarked upon one of its fastest growth periods. It was synonymous with loads of opportunity. As a result, net immigration into the United States from around the world and particularly poorer economies in Europe was extraordinarily large. That's because the economic opportunities were here in the United States. But, that period would come to a very abrupt end, and one of the most important ends in all of economic history. It came to an end in an event that really shook the foundations of our ideas about what makes a classical economy work, about this whole self-correcting idea, and about what it is that makes an economy successful and what a good government does in an economy that's unsuccessful. That period of growth ended in what we now call the Great Depression.

The Great Depression is great. It is not a recession. It is not a small event. It's Krakatau in economic terms. It's a giant black hole that squats in the middle of U.S. economic history and demands to be explained. It demanded to be explained so much that it destroyed a lot of the theories that people held to fast in the early part of the 20th century. From the Great Depression, we get an entirely new view of economics and what it takes to govern a modern macro economy.

The idea that really shook the foundations of people with the Great Depression was that the world's largest economy could collapse and completely collapse after a decade of growth. During the Great Depression, the U.S. went from having an unemployment rate of only about 5% to an unemployment rate of 25% and more in certain areas. Across the nation, at least 1/4 of every able-bodied worker couldn't find work. It wasn't that they couldn't find work for a month or 3 months or 6 months, many of them for years couldn't find work. Not only in the United States was this depression felt, world trade flows fell by half around the world. Stock prices fell in 1929 to a level so far 2 years later that it took 25 years for the stock market to return to the levels that they had achieved prior to the beginning of the Great Depression. It's an extraordinary event that changed not only the way we think about the economy but the way people live and think about their lives ever since.

Hard as it is to do, let's forget about what exactly caused the Great Depression. That's really important, but let's think about why it was so great—what made it a Great Depression and not just another recession, because after all, recessions are really commonplace. There's nothing about a short period of economic fall that really is inconsistent with a classical economy just re-equilibrating. Recessions are common, and they're not inconsistent with anyone's beliefs about what it means to be healthy. But the Great Depression was different. It lasted; or rather, it just wouldn't go away. There was no self-correction. The Great Depression really challenged the idea that the economy would self-equilibrate. Sure there were 25% of the people unemployed, but what was happening to wages? Why wouldn't they fall low enough to bring people back to work? There was all this fall in the stock market. Companies failed, prices collapsed, and yet it just kept getting worse and worse. There seemed to be no bottom, and that really shook the foundations of faith in the U.S. economy and in free markets in general.

You can think about it in another way. A belief in self-correction really translates into a belief in the price adjustment process. Countries don't go out of business; they're not like companies. If prices fall too far and a company can't make its payroll, it collapses. But, countries don't work that way. When prices fall, people just accept lower wages. They go back to work at lower wages and it hurts, but everybody gets back on board, or so it would seem. Prices adjust and normally that ultimately puts people back into the workforce, except when it doesn't happen. Fundamental to this classical economical idea was this idea that supply would create its own demand, this idea that if you produce something, eventually you could sell it. There wouldn't be this enduring inventory of anything for too long. Eventually you could lower a price to a certain level, and there would be demand. Really, classical economical ideas were just about how rapidly prices could adjust. It might be painful, but it would work, and an economy would once again be able to grow when prices moved to the right level. There was no such thing as a viscous circle from which you couldn't escape. But, the Great Depression showed that this really wasn't true, or at least it showed that we didn't understand economies in the way that we thought we would.

John Maynard Keynes really captured this idea when he said, "In the long run, we're all dead." What he meant by that was (this was a retort to classical economists) it might be that in the long run the economy self-corrects itself, but if it self-corrects over a period of 10 years, who really cares? That's so long that the pain and suffering endured in the process of self-correction is too much to bear. Keynes said we had a failure of aggregate demand. What we needed was not just some price adjustment to stimulate one market, to stimulate one economy or one region, but some grander action. It was really the birth of the idea that a government in this situation should not sit still, should not wait for prices to self-equilibrate. It should act. It should do something to get the economy back on track.

You also had this great problem in the Depression of this viscous circle. For Keynes this viscous circle is probably best and closely aligned with the idea of deflation, especially the idea that prices could keep falling year in and year out. Think of it this way. If you were planning to buy a car and suddenly you heard a rumor that prices on cars were going to fall the next week, what would you do? I'm pretty sure you'd wait that week out. But, what if at the end of that week, or let's say a day before that week ended, someone said,

I think prices are going to fall even further? Then, you'd wait even longer. Because expectations could travel in this negative way, that a belief that prices would fall would lead people to hold back purchases, and so therefore perhaps cause prices to fall even further, you seem to have an economy that had no bottom. This was a problem that Keynes really tried to work out. It's also a problem that led to something we'll discuss in subsequent lectures, which is about monetary policy and the role of the Federal Reserve Board and other central banks. In a situation when prices are falling, what should they do?

The lessons of the Great Depression were hard to learn. Parts of the lessons were good lessons and some of them were hard to adapt in ways that really made the economy better off. In some ways, we learned how to solve problems of the Great Depression by acting with banking insurance and by putting people to work, and by having a government that acted in a very heavy way. Some would argue that these are negative things, in fact, and to some degree they come with their downside, but they seem to help in the process. The U.S. economy adapted to the Great Depression in the ways that it always adapted just as it adapted at the end of the 19th century by regulating monopolies and creating institutions to govern the economy and create a better safety net.

The U.S. wouldn't be challenged again in that way until about 2007 when the next great crisis began. That great crisis, which began as something called the Sub Prime Crisis, really began because—it's odd—it didn't begin because the United States was so weak. It really in some sense began because the United States was so strong. In fact, I'd say that its strength became its weakness. It was such a strong economy, there was so much confidence placed in the United States, that the money flows came easy from around the world. Because the money came in easily, it was used sloppily, and that was the seeds of the beginning of one of the greatest recessions in U.S. history.

You can think about it in some simple ways. Savings rates in the United States were really always much lower than they were in pure economies. What does that really reflect? It certainly reflects lots of things. But one of the reasons that people had relatively low savings in the United States is because they were really confident. You might save a lot if you're worried about your future, but if you're not worried about it at all or if you just have a lot of confidence, you don't need to save that much. It wasn't that there was a high penalty for not saving or a high reward to saving, because in the early part of the 20<sup>th</sup> century, interest rates in the United States were lower than ever despite the fact that everyone was spending as much as ever, and there was no savings. It's because money was flowing in so readily from around the world that the United States could live without saving for itself and seemingly without paying a penalty for not saving.

Why did this occur? Why did people become so confident that they failed to save? Why did they take all that money and put it into houses, houses whose values rose unreasonably high and fast, houses that were backed by mortgages and banks that had such confidence in the strength and infallibility of the U.S. economy that they never thought all that seriously about this house of cards crumbling down? How did we overlook that?

The first reason is that it became easy to look only at the short run. The idea that one needed to look further than 2 or 3 years into the future didn't seem to strike anybody as all that important. One of the reasons that's true is because most of us bought into a very old classical idea about rational investors or an idea that investors knew better than anyone else what they needed to do to protect themselves. What is a rational investor? A rational investor is one that looks forward, thinks about all the risks, makes a careful decision, really hedges their bets, and thinks about all the potential consequences that they could face. But, in the U.S., it seemed that things were too good. We had such confidence in the stability of our system that we really never thought about that.

In fact, for about 20 years leading up to the recession that began in 2007, the U.S. had really had only 3/4 of negative economic growth. Things had been so good for so long that no one really seemed to think they needed to be long-sighted. They could think about the next few months, the next few days in fact. If those days turned out great, it was all the more reason to be more confident and to lever up and to bet more on the system.

The real problem isn't that no one ever thought about investors behaving irrationally. We think that in most times they think more or less rationally and that people are careful. The real problem is trying to understand how people act when they behave irrationally. You might think of it this way: There's sort of one way to think rationally, but there's an infinite number of ways to be irrational. How do we know which one to base our economic policies on? How do we know how people's irrational behavior will aggregate up into some net effect on the economy? We didn't really understand that. For that reason, we've never really understood how economic manias take place, how housing booms and asset bubbles really come to have life, and how even in the midst of it—when everyone's looking around thinking this is crazy, isn't it, this can't go on forever—no one seems to have the guts or the ability to hold back and stop it. It's a runaway train and it's something that lots of economies face. It's certainly something that the U.S. economy faced in the beginning of 2007 and for the next couple of years.

We didn't really react very carefully to all those global capital inflows. One could've asked a similar question: Why is the world so anxious, so willing, so ready to lend the U.S. economy, one that doesn't save, one that is inhabited by lots of reckless behavior and lots of reckless investors? Why was all the money flowing to this one place? They weren't necessarily behaving rationally, but there wasn't enough questioned about that. Perhaps there was not enough a belief that, if those global capital flows reverse quickly, the United States would have a heavy price to pay. It would need to react quickly, perhaps more quickly than it was able to react.

How did we react when the global capital flows began to shake, when the bubble began to burst, and when it finally became painfully obvious that this extraordinary rise in housing prices could not be sustained? How did we react as the economy crumbled, as unemployment mounted, as pessimism spread, as profits fell? We reacted in a very aggressive way, in some part by taking the lessons of the Great Depression. If you look back at the Depression, most criticisms say we either didn't react well or we reacted too mildly. Even the massive programs of President Roosevelt weren't enough to lift the economy out of the Great Depression. It's taken as a sign of truth that everyone knows that only the Second World War really ended the Great Depression. It took a stimulus on that scale to really move this large economy into a healthy state again. In taking that lesson and in taking another lesson about controlling the money supply and making sure that it doesn't shrink, did we react in the most massive way in all of economic history? In the United States in 2008 and in the months that passed and in 2009, the United States engaged in the most massive government stimulus and break from self-correction in all of economic history.

There are just a few simple ways. The United States first reacted by doubling the money supply. That's literally taking the stock of money from which all the currency you and I hold is based and doubling it in about a week. That's an extraordinary event, but it was all designed to support a banking system and to create confidence to ensure people that banks wouldn't fail. We enacted legislation that led to over a trillion dollars of economic stimulus. That's a trillion with a T, and if you don't know it, that's a thousand billion or a million million. It's a very big number, big enough one would hope, and this was part of the aim, to create confidence. If they're spending a trillion dollars, surely this must work. In short, we reacted in a very status way that represents a full break from purely classical or even neoclassical ideas about self-correction. This is in large part a bridge from free markets and crisis to something that begins to look or that one might describe as a bit more socialist. It's a huge bet. It's in fact the biggest bet ever, and it's the result of ideas from John Maynard Keynes to Milton Friedman. If it's right, we'll have learned the lessons of the Great Depression, we will have applied the solutions we didn't know to apply then, and we'll have avoided that pain for a second time. But, if in fact it proves to be wrong and there are longer-term consequences to the United States, then it will no longer be what it has been, the leading economic light of the world and a free-market economy, one and one with the old idea perhaps of the American dream.

If it works, we might get some inflation and we might get lots of debt, and if it doesn't, we'll get lots of debt and stagnation and unemployment. Just as during the Great Depression we needed to re-imagine solutions, we'll need to re-imagine solutions to the great recession that began in 2007. Either way, we're looking at problems that none of us have worried about for decades.

It's going to come down to our behavior and whether we'll see hope and confidence and reasons to stimulate and act aggressively again. It's going to come down to the confidence of the people and the ideas that they have about their own economy and whether they have faith in it. Whether, from internally and externally, people look at the United States and still see that leading free-market economy of the world. That economy, that from at least 1870 to the present day, has been the ultimate concept of free markets, the ultimate concept of growth and productivity. We don't know what's going to happen to the U.S., and we never have at any point in time. We have lots of reasons to hope and lots of lessons to have been learned, but do we know if they're the right ones? Do we know if they're going to be the solutions that will lead us out of the recession of 2007? Unfortunately, only time will tell as it always does. But, if there's one thing that holds the U.S. together and there's one thing that we hope holds all free-market economies together, it's the idea that we can adapt to any problem. With enough time and enough aggressive behavior, we can lead ourselves out of any economic problem. At least we hope it'll be true this time.

# America and Europe—Divergent Approaches
## Lecture 6

One of the most significant outcomes of this divergence in path at the end of the Second World War was on the risk-bearing borne by individuals and by the populations of each country. In Western Europe, the government began to take more rein and bear more risk; in the United States, more of those risks were left to the individual.

At the end of the Second World War, a "Western divide" emerged between the United States and its peer economies in Western Europe. At the beginning of the war, the economies of Western Europe and the United States had reached somewhat similar levels of development. After the war, Europe was devastated, while the United States was launched into mega-power status. It was during this period that the economies of Western Europe and the United States started down different ideological and performance paths.

The economic policies that Europeans had followed before the Second World War grew more entrenched and more prominent after the war. Broadly speaking, European nations grew toward deeper government involvement in most aspects of the economies—in particular, in the provision of a social safety net and the regulation of business. The United States grew its social safety net, as well, but it also sharpened the connections between individual success and individual effort.

The economies of Western Europe moved in three basic directions that separated them from the United States. First, the Western European economies aggressively integrated across borders. This move enabled the sharing of production in order to lower costs, expand the resource base, and generate more peaceful interactions between nations. Second, European nations greatly strengthened their support for the unemployed. Finally, they greatly expanded healthcare benefits and subsidies for education.

Throughout this period of divergence, for the most part, the economies of Western Europe and that of the United States performed well. Their relative performance, however, reinforced much of our thinking about what it takes to succeed economically and what the costs are of providing extensive social benefits. What we saw in Western Europe that differentiated it from the United States was a divergence in the natural level of unemployment and slower economic growth. In Western Europe, ever since the end of the Second World War, we see relatively higher unemployment than in the United States, higher tax rates, and slower economic growth.

**[After the Second World War,] rather than let businesses produce what they want when they want to sell to whom they want at what price they want, Europeans embarked upon a road of more government regulation, more limitations on private business, a real firm break from very classical ideas.**

Unlike the European Union, the United States engaged in a social system of sharper incentives for productivity, a weaker social safety net, and greater penalties for being unemployed. As we know from previous lectures, people respond to incentives, and here, they responded exactly as we might think. They worked harder, they took more risks, and they worked longer hours than their counterparts in Western Europe. As a result, there was more production, the economy grew faster, and the income distribution grew wider.

What was the result of the divergence? In the United States, we had income levels that were naturally higher than those in Europe throughout this entire period. At the same time, we had greater economic inequality. The answer to the question of which approach is "better" boils down to more of a social choice than an economic one: How much of a tradeoff is a society willing to make between productivity and economic growth on the one hand and income inequality on the other? ∎

## Suggested Reading

Friedman and Schwartz, *A Monetary History of the United States.*
Keynes, *The Economic Consequences of the Peace.*
———. *The General Theory of Employment, Interest and Money.*
Yergin and Stanislaw, *The Commanding Heights.*

## Questions to Consider

1. What was the economic tradeoff made by European nations after World War II? Was it worth it?

2. Is growth the paramount goal of economic policy? How should it be balanced with other economic and social objectives?

# America and Europe—Divergent Approaches
## Lecture 6—Transcript

Welcome back. In the previous lecture, we took a hard look at the United States and what's led to its successes and its adaptations over the many years that it's reigned supreme over the world economy. We understand that the United States is in some sense a very special economy, but it's also among peers. It's not so different from its peers that it's completely different. Yet beginning at the middle part of the 20th century there emerges this Western divide. We want to understand that Western divide and what separates the United States from its peer economies in Western Europe.

The first thing we can say about the Western divide and the period of time when the United States seemed to peel away and began to look much more different than its peers than ever before is that it all really began at the end of the Second World War. In fact the Second World War made it a huge difference. It really separated the United States and the European Union in a very fundamental way. That's not to say that they weren't different before, but it is to say that after the Second World War we really begin to think about these being 2 very different economic systems and economic approaches. That's an overstatement to be sure—they're really more like cousins—but after the Second World War these look like very different economies and for very good reasons.

The United States really began its reign as the leading economy of the world long before the start of the 20th century and therefore long before the Second World War. But its true dominance, its real mega power status, really coincides with the end of that Second World War. It's actually very easy to understand why that's true. The outcomes of the war on the domestic economy of the United States stood in very stark contrast to the outcomes on those of all the other major combatants who were also economic peers at the time. Think about the outcomes in the war on the economies of Western Europe, the places where the battles took place, of Japan, the place in Asia where the other big part of the war took place, and in the United States where no battles took place on domestic soil and where it was the ultimate victor and the largest economy standing at the end.

What we can say is that the economies of Western Europe and the United States, and even Japan, had reached somewhat similar levels of economic development by the beginning of the war. That's not to say that they weren't the same, that's not just saying that they didn't already have many of the characteristics that they would come to see and that we would come to see after the war, but they were much more similar before the war than after the war. Before the Second World War, it's true that continental Europeans and other European nations were already more socially liberal. They already offered more of a social safety net, something they would come to do more of after the Second World War. It's true also that after the Great Depression, the United States moved closer in that direction toward offering more of a social safety net, but it was still a largely open free-market, classical, competitive economy that had relatively little government intervention or support.

After the Second World War, Europe was mostly devastated. In fact, its largest economies were very much destroyed, at least their manufacturing capabilities were destroyed by the war. Take Germany, for example, the largest European economy absolutely devastated by the war. Take Great Britain, take France—also devastated by the war. It's not just the fact that these were some of the world's largest economies and most successful economies and peers of the United States; they were also peers of the United States in production. They were also peers and competitors in the commercial world as much as they were combatants and allies of the marshal world of the Second World War.

There was also the basic problem after the war of sustaining an economy in transition from a heavy warlike posture. This often happens in war, but the demand to sustain the economies of Western Europe and the United States was gone at the end of the war, and this is always what happens. Most nations to fight a war actually experience a period of economic growth or at least higher values of output, and there's a pretty simple reason for that. In order to muster together the resources, the tanks, the guns, the ships, and the planes that you need to fight a war, most economies go into debt. They need human resources and physical resources to make all these armaments. What they do is lever up the economy and expand production in ways that generally grow the economy during the war, but once they're gone, actually let the economy deflate. Most economies in post-war periods are in a period of transition toward a more stable non-wartime posture. It can be very difficult.

In Western Europe, this is a really difficult process because they had to engage upon a massive rebuilding effort, a massive effort to rebuild commercial capabilities, so that they could produce, so that they could compete with the West and their other neighbors and the United States. By contrast, the United States was a victor in a contest that really devastated most of its commercial competitors around the world and its nearest economic rivals. The United States was also very heavily in debt. In fact, the debt to gross domestic product ratio, one of the standard measures of the indebtedness of a country, had gone from about a third of GDP to a little over 100% of GDP. During that period of the Second World War, the United States was massively in debt. Even though it was in debt, at the end of the Second World War, it was the absolute undisputed center of the global economy. It also produced the world's chief currency, the U.S. dollar, the currency that really sustained all economic transactions of the world. There's always one, and the United States was not only the leading economy of the world, but it produced the monetary equivalent of gold that was used everywhere and was all-important.

It's really during this period at the end of the Second World War that the 2 economies, if you will, that the different economies of Western Europe and the economy of the United States, began down these largely different ideological paths and these different performance paths. These would demarcate these economic ideologies of a more socialist, but free-market approach and a more pure free-market open-economy approach in the United States. These ideologies seemed different enough that we always talk about them as if they're very different. They're related, but these are 2 variants. If you will, they are 2 grand experiments that we embarked upon at the end of the Second World War and which enable us to compare the performance of the economies in ways that teach us about economics, macroeconomics, and which is a better way to live, the European way or the economic way of the United States. Which was better, which worked better? These are all questions that that change enables us to begin to answer.

One change is largely true—the economic policies that Europeans were following before the Second World War really grew more entrenched and really became more present after the Second World War. Broadly speaking, European economies grew toward far more deep government involvement in most aspects of the economy—in particular, in the provision of a social safety net and in the regulation of business. For example, today when we associate economic standards and economic standards demarcated by government, we think about Europeans. Europeans have much stricter environmental standards, for example, standards that limit the activities of business to limit the impact of those business activities on the overall human environment and physical environment. They also have standards about what products are safe that are more strict than those we see in the United States and in most other countries of the world. They have standards, for example, around foodstuffs and what we'd call sanitary or phytosanitary standards of foods to help make sure that people are healthy. That is, rather than let businesses produce what they want when they want to sell to whom they want at what price they want, Europeans embarked upon a road of more government regulation, more limitations on private business, a real firm break from very classical ideas.

It's not to say that the U.S. didn't also move somewhat in that direction; it also grew its social safety net slowly and modestly, but it also sharpened the connections. It sharpened incentives for performance. It sharpened the connections between individual successes and individual effort. While it also offered something more of a safety net, it actually also stretched the boundaries between rich and poor, between success and failure, in ways that were much more consistent with a move toward more free-market economic beliefs. The economies of Western Europe moved in 3 basic directions that really separated them from the United States, that really demarcated the difference between a Western European socialist approach and an American-style free-market approach. These 3 areas really held sway for all of the post-war period through the end of the 20th century and continue to teach us a little bit about what it is that really creates a difference in economic living standards and how we might begin to make sensible choices about how to live and what the cost of those choices are on our economic performance.

The first big difference that Western European economies embarked upon was that they integrated across borders in a very aggressive way. It actually began kind of slowly. After the end of the Second World War, Western European economies needed production. They needed more to sustain themselves. They were reeling and recovering and slowly getting back on their feet and establishing firmer economic fundamentals. What they realized is what all businesses realize, that sometimes it's cheaper to operate on large scales than it is to operate on small scales. They wanted to find ways to integrate across borders and share production in a productive way that would not only perhaps lower cost, expand the resource base, but maybe even generate a little more peaceful interactions between nations that had fought each other.

They began with something called the European Coal and Steel Community, which was really just a confederation of a few markets that said we're going to trade coal and steel across our borders more freely than ever before. This European Coal and Steel Community actually became the European common market. In 1960, it was born through the Treaty of Rome. Eventually, this integration across borders, this confederation of countries, would become the European Union that we know today—the real integration of the economies of Western Europe in what one might call a United States of Europe or a much more integrated global economy in that one region of the world.

One could argue that the U.S. had already gone down that path. In fact, you could think about the states of the United States as being different economies and it's true that they were already very integrated. But, these cooperative international policies that were seen in Europe really represented something more than just integration across state borders. They represented a real diminishment of an identity of a single national economy. They were the beginning of an identity of a European economy, of a trans-border trans-cultural economy, the likes of which the world had really not seen in the modern era.

As a part of that change, as a part of that integration across borders, it was also required that these economies were more open to each other. That's a difficult thing to do, but they opened up and lowered their restrictions in a very pronounced and effective way over many decades. That openness required some conformity of policies across countries that previously had very different policies, maybe policies about what made you a doctor or policies about what was legal and what was legal in production or what were legal wages or legal ways to treat people in the workforce or out of the workforce.

Politically, in order to integrate policies and to have similar policies, Europeans generally found it easier to average up restrictions. That is, if we needed to have conformist polices, if we needed to have all the same policy in France and in Germany and in Belgium and in Great Britain, it was easier to take the most restrictive policy and average up to that than it was to really force everyone to really lower their policies to the lowest level. What we see in this integration across borders is the averaging up of economic restrictions on business and, in general, on economic open trade policies outside of the European Union. Politically this was a difficult push, but it made the social safety net stronger, not weaker. It made the support that governments provided individuals and the restrictions they placed upon business larger and stronger, not smaller. Particularly in Germany and France, people wanted greater economic security and being large economies the policies of these economies seemed to hold sway.

The second big change that we saw in European nations after the end of the Second World War was that they greatly strengthened their support for the unemployed. They already had relatively strong support for the unemployed, but they strengthened them in a very big way, offering more holidays, higher pay, more restrictions on when you could fire someone for cause or even for not cause, more opportunities for advancement, more training, and more protections in a legal sense. The U.S. in fact also followed along in a somewhat similar fashion, but the base of economic protections for workers in the U.S. was already a good deal lower than it was in Europe prior to the beginning of the Second World War. Afterward, those protections really grew further apart, even though the United States was also raising its protections. Throughout the post-war period, we see much stronger support for the unemployed—stronger and higher unemployment pay, fewer hours of work, and greater protections within the workplace.

In fact, this is one of the starkest differences between the U.S. and the European Union that last from the post-war period through the end of the 20th century. European levels of unemployment insurance were also bolstered by rising union powers. Unions had been strong in the United States, were even stronger in Western Europe, but they really diverged a bit after the end of the Second World War. Unions remained very strong in Europe and grew much weaker in the United States. Along with union power came work guarantees, guarantees of employment, minimum wages that were high, protection, and nothing like employment at will, which allows an employer to fire a worker for almost no cause whatsoever. This was unheard of in Europe and the divergence between the economies became very stark around this issue of support for the unemployed.

Moreover, people just began to work less in Europe over this period of time. If we look at the average weekly work hours in Europe at the end of the Second World War and compare them to the average weekly work hours in Europe at the end of the 20th century, we see a dramatic fall—a fall from over 40 hours per week on average to a little bit less than 34 hours per week and as low as 32 hours per week in some economies. It's just a lot less work, and that was part and parcel of this support for the unemployed. You might think of this as the beginning of some blunter incentives around workers in greater Europe. There was more protection, a little bit less work, and less threat of losing one's job if one worked less than they did before.

As a result, firms in Europe actually had a harder time competing in the global marketplace, particularly large firms. They were far more constrained than their U.S. counterparts when it came to managing the workforce in all the associated costs. They couldn't fire workers, they couldn't force them to work longer hours, and to many in most of Western Europe, this was a great hindrance. At least to many employers it was a great hindrance. Most employees seem to have a very different opinion and, as a result, politically these were very popular moves.

Thirdly, European nations were very different from the U.S. in the following way. They greatly expanded healthcare benefits and subsidies for education. It's true, just as with other examples, the U.S. also moved somewhat in this direction. There were greater advances and greater support for healthcare, and there were greater programs that enabled people to go to school who previously couldn't afford it. But really the differences grew large. In particular in Western Europe, most economies adopted full-scale complete universal health coverage of some kind. That wasn't without consequences, but it did change the nature of the relationship between individuals and their security around healthcare and in the relationship between the state and what it provided individuals. Healthcare was no longer seen as something that was not a right of an individual; it was a right, and government had the right to step in to provide it.

The same is true for tertiary education or college education. In most of Western Europe, there was a fairly strong move to providing college education at low or even no cost. This was greatly different than in the United States. While the United States had some programs supporting tertiary education, for the most part college education remained for profit, private institutions, and some state-led institutions but certainly not free.

Through this different period for both economies, through this great divergence at the end of the Second World War, for the most part both of the economies, that is, the economies of Western Europe and the economies of the United States, performed very well. They were largely positive periods. They were rich economies at the beginning, and they were still rich at the end. But their relative performance did enforce a lot of our thinking about what it takes to succeed economically and what the costs are of providing social provisions like healthcare and almost free tertiary education. One of the most significant outcomes of this divergence in path at the end of the Second World War was on the risk bearing borne by individuals and by the populations of each country. In Western Europe, the government began to take more reign and bear more risk; in the United States, more of those risks were left to the individual.

It's actually pretty simple: The greater social protections that were added in Western Europe were popular, they were seen as enlightened, but they were also really expensive and costly. As a result, governments had to step up and provide more of these. They had to increase taxes. What we saw in Western Europe that really differentiated them at the end of the Second World War from the United States was a divergence in the natural level of unemployment and slower economic growth. In Western Europe, ever since the end of the Second World War, we see relatively higher unemployment than in the United States and slower economic growth. It's not exactly slow, at least not in most periods, but notably slower in 3 big differences. We see higher tax rates in the European Union. You had to have them. In order to cover the increase cost of the social safety net, you have to have higher taxes. We can begin to see how higher taxes on individuals might reduce incentives for people to work really hard. You could think the reverse, but in fact if it's an income tax, and I take less home from my paycheck, perhaps I have even less incentive to work hard.

This led to something that most labeled as Euro-sclerosis, this sickness in the European economies. It wasn't that they weren't treating people better or even responding politically to great and reasonable demands, but it was the fact that we had a fairly predictable impact on that economy. Higher tax rates, the social safety net, stronger benefits for the unemployed, lower ability of managers, and managers of large firms in particular, to encourage productivity in the workplace, led to higher unemployment levels. In fact, for a large fraction of the post-war period, unemployment levels in Western Europe are about 2 times that of the United States, at least at the highest. That's a significant level and one that endured year in and year out. The third major result is that economic growth was notably slower. None of these economies were what we might think of as very fast growing over this period, but there was a clear difference, a statistically significant difference, between the economic growth rate of the United States and the economic growth rate that we saw in Western Europe.

What we began to see were the average income levels in the Western European economies were notably lower, and they weren't converging on the U.S. A gap opened, it winded a bit, and it endured. But, we also saw something else. Even though income levels were lower, we saw that the distribution of income in Western Europe remained a bit tighter than in the United States. The differences between the very rich and the very poor in Western Europe might have been stark to some, but they didn't really grow wider. In the United States they did. The rich did get richer, but the poor didn't really get richer at the same rate and so the gap widened. It wasn't the old case of the Great Depression where they used to say the rich get richer and the poor get children. The rich did get richer and the poor more or less stayed the same, but this difference really is exaggerated in the United States in a way that's more or less consistent with what we would expect from free-market stories.

It really works in the following way. Think about it this way. What the U.S. really did that was different than the European Union is it engaged in a social system of sharper incentives for productivity, a weaker social safety net, and greater penalties for being unemployed. It's a predictable effect. With more penalties for being unemployed, with higher income levels for those that can earn them and lower taxes on all those profits, you have a system of much sharper incentives to be productive and successful. As we remember from previous lectures, people respond to incentives. In the United States they responded exactly as you think they would. They worked harder, they took more risk, and they worked longer hours than their counterparts in Western Europe. As a result, there was more production, the economy grew faster, and the income distribution grew wider—a fairly natural result and something that these 2 economies help us prove. Sharper incentives do tend to work at the macroeconomic level. In economies that are simpler, sharper incentives lead to faster growth and a wider distribution of income and that's the tradeoff. It's something that we really learn in this bold experiment these 2 economies embark upon at the end of the Second World War.

What do we have as a result? In the United States, you have something that you might really like. You have income levels that were naturally higher in Europe throughout this entire period. It's true, the United States is not only a larger economy than any single economy in Western Europe, it's also generally richer, and it stays that way. That seems a natural result of these sharper incentives and a weaker social safety net.

You might think of an interpretation like this: Free markets do tend to work or at least the freeing of markets and the imposing of sharper incentives on individuals do work the way that we think they do. They encourage productivity. They lead to human behaviors that invest more in action and invest more in work that take more risk, and that leads to greater economic growth. In some sense, it confirms the basis for freeing of markets. It does lead to faster growth.

But, the flipside of these strong incentives are in fact more unequal outcomes, and that's exactly what we got in the U.S.—an economy that moved to faster growth but also much more unequal living standards. It's hard to understand whether or not that tradeoff is absolutely necessary, but it is the one that we would predict from economic theory. Sharper incentives lead to more productivity and greater economic inequality, or at least they did in the U.S.

Looking forward, what does this really mean? What does this really tell us about which economic system is better or how these 2 economies will fair, whether or not one approach is better than the other? We might think of it this way: It seems to be largely a choice of how societies choose to live and how much of a tradeoff between productivity and economic growth and income equality, or perhaps inequality, we're actually willing to make. In some sense, we might think it's not so much an economic choice as it is a social one. For example, we could ask the following: In Western European nations, we see blunter incentives. When I say blunter incentives, I mean less of an incentive to work hard. You don't have the same sort of unemployment problem. For example, in Western Europe, an unemployed person might have benefits for being unemployed for any reason for up to 6 months. Certainly benefits that accrue to individuals who are taking maternity leave or paternity leave are twice as large or more so in Western Europe. That may be a socially good thing, but it's also what we might think of as a much blunter incentive to be productive. It's a blunter incentive to stay and work and to keep earning an income because, if you're not working, the penalty isn't as high.

Contrast that to what you see in the United States. If one is unemployed in the United States and in most non-union shops and in most states around the United States, you can be out of work and stay out of work for a long period of time. Unemployment might cover the first 6 weeks or so; after that, you're on your own. Do we think about those blunter incentives in Europe being worth it? Do we think about them being predictable? In some sense, yes they are predictable. They do lead to lower economic productivity and lower economic incomes and a greater level of natural unemployment, but that's the tradeoff and we all seem to understand that.

In some ways, we can look at some specific examples and see how this is true. It's not just that these differences occur at a national level; we can look at specific industries or even a sector of the economy. One way to look at this and one way that helps us contextualize these tradeoffs is to think about the different university systems or national university systems that we tend to see in both regions of the world. It's an intriguing example of how these 2 models matter and how these tradeoffs are really borne out. For example, in the United States, we tend to have private universities and public universities, but both of them actually charge amply for their products and their services. In fact, we've seen in the United States the cost of college education really rise, but we also see much higher incomes for administrators and professors in colleges and universities in the United States. Colleges and universities in the United States have a greater freedom to hire and to fire. As a result, they've tended to pay larger incomes to more of the world's best scientists and have tended to have more successful universities as a whole, at least if you regard success as having greater minds, more research expenditures, and faster growth.

In Western Europe, we see quite the opposite. Private institutions in the United States and private colleges have led the pack, have led to a supremacy in economic power, at least as it relates to the economic power and the performance of universities and colleges. The supremacy in the United States has mattered a lot. It's been the seabed for a lot of growth and innovation. One could argue that it's the result of having sharper incentives and institutions for performance, a greater ability to fire, to charge one's own prices. It should work for productivity, and it seems to have mattered in the university setting. It also means that the cost of education in the United States is much higher, that it's more rationed and less available, but that's the tradeoff that we seem to get.

That means that the risks borne in an economy where we have these sharper incentives are predictable. They work in the way that we think, but are they sustainable? Will it still be that the economy that succeeds in the latter part of the 20th century will be the type of economy that's going to succeed in the future? Perhaps it's the case that individuals understand these risks and are willing to accept them in the context of the United States, but not so much in others. We might begin to ask ourselves which economy and which way of living is really best suited for the realities of growth in a flatter much more volatile world of the 21st century. That's a difficult question to answer, but what our economies teaches us and what these 2 examples teach us is that these things work out in the way we might predict. Sharper incentives lead to more behavior consistent with productivity and growth and more inequality.

In closing, we could say that what we see in this great experiment of the post-war economies of Western Europe and the United States are 2 stories,

2 stories that evidence how incentives for human behavior matter, and they matter in a way that lead to vastly different ways of living. The differences in the average growth rates between these 2 regions are actually relatively small, but we know that over time small differences matter a lot, and we know how they're going to matter. That still doesn't help us to answer perhaps the most fundamental question, the one that we started with and the one we still can't answer: What's the better way to live? What's the better economy? In some degree what we can do as economists is to accentuate and to explain the tradeoffs. The answer to which way is better, that's a matter of taste, and we know there's no accounting for that.

# State-Led Theories of Economic Growth
## Lecture 7

Growth is really all about economic productivity—full stop. That's it. If you achieve productivity growth, which is the ability to take resources and extract more value from them over time, if you can continue that process, in some ways, it doesn't matter how you get there as long as you get there.

In Lecture 2, we asked the question: How fast is fast when it comes to economic growth? In answering that question, we found a puzzle: Some of the best-performing economies are those in which there is heavy government involvement—quite different from the classical policies that led to the Western economic miracle. Could it be that free markets don't have as much to do with growth as we think?

To answer that question, we look at Japan, uncontested as a speed demon for growth. Between 1950 and 1973, nominal GDP in Japan was regularly growing at more than 10 percent per year. Between 1965 and 1970, real growth—real buying power of individuals—averaged nearly 11 percent per year. How did Japan manage to grow at such a rapid rate for such a long period of time?

The story of a low-income economy catching up to a high-income economy was first described by Robert Solo, a Nobel Prize–winning economist. According to Solo, a backward nation can actually grow at a much faster rate than a highly developed one. The economic and technological leaders, such as the United States and the nations of Western Europe, buck the headwinds, so to speak, of technological advance, and those behind, if they have the ability, can copy those advances and catch up much more quickly.

Japan was able to make its great economic leap for a number of reasons. First, there was heavy cooperation and planning between business and government. The government subsidized such firms as Toyota, Honda, and Sony and structured favorable export policies, while ensuring that those firms didn't have significant domestic competition. A second key to Japan's success was that the nation had very high savings rates, not only by individuals but also in government and business. This enabled investment in education and infrastructure and kept the value of the yen low, making Japanese products even more competitive in international markets.

In some sense, Japan is the prototypical example of a state-led government economy, which would seem to contradict our story that the free market is golden. What lessons can we learn here? One truth is that growth is really about economic productivity—total production—and nothing else. And if we divide all economic activity into three "buckets," we can begin to understand where productivity comes from and how it relates to different government approaches. The first bucket is the labor force, the second is the employment level, and the third and most important is average worker productivity. Japan had favorable conditions in all three buckets.

**By 25 years after the end of the Second World War, a war that devastated their economy, [the Japanese] were really back on top. They were really back at the top of world income levels and living at income levels that were only enjoyed by a select few rich nations.**

Perhaps the takeaway here is that high investments, funded by high savings, generated and supported by an economy with political stability and a workforce that's growing in skill, results in more productive people throughout the economy—even without the free-market approach. But that higher average worker productivity is hard to sustain, and the fact is that after 40 years of growth, around 1990, Japan entered its own great depression. The good news is that Japan is largely back on track, and it has, to some degree, regained much of the stability it lost in the period of the 1990s to at least the year 2000. ■

## Important Term

**average worker productivity**: Calculated by dividing total economic output (GDP) by the number of employed workers in an economy.

## Suggested Reading

Friedman and Schwartz, *A Monetary History of the United States.*

Helpman, *The Mystery of Economic Growth.*

Kindleberger, *The World in Depression.*

Yergin and Stanislaw, *The Commanding Heights.*

## Questions to Consider

1. How was Japan able to sustain high growth rates long after its recovery from the devastation of World War II? What did the Japanese do that can be copied elsewhere?

2. Was the Japanese miracle evidence of a different economic model of growth?

# State-Led Theories of Economic Growth
## Lecture 7—Transcript

A few lectures back we asked the question how fast is fast when it comes to economic growth. Our objective in asking that question was really straightforward. If we want to look at examples of success, then we have to know which economies were successful. To know which economies were successful, we need to be able to answer that question—how fast is fast. Once we answer that question, we can use economic history to show us where to look for economic successes and to learn from the winners, and in fact to learn from the losers about this quest for economic development and perhaps prescribe better smarter policies. Without the ability to do experiments, which economists at this level don't really have, this is really the best that we can do.

In that process, we actually found a puzzle. That puzzle was this: Economies that were run by states or where there was a heavy hand of government involvement, those that seemed to break the classic rules of the Western economic miracle that seemed in some ways very different from the policies that led to the great success in the United States, those economies are some of the best performing economies in history, at least for a period of time, and this is a problem that we have to resolve. It really forces us to think about this fundamental question. Could it be that free markets don't have as much to do with growth as we think, or could it be that we misunderstand them after all?

If we want to try to answer that question, we can look at one of the experiments in economic history that most closely is associated with the shaking of that foundation, that foundation that links free markets and the Western economic miracle to the fundamentals that actually lead to all economic growth. That place to look is Japan. Japan in economic terms is the absolute uncontested speed demon for growth. If we ask how fast is fast again, we could say this: Fast is an economy where the incomes of the people in it grow in inflation adjusted or what we call real terms by about 8–9% per year for about 20 years in a row. You have to think about that for a minute and not just think about this being abstract, but think about being there. That's 20 years in a row of growing 8–9% per year on top of any inflation number; that's fast and that's a Japanese level of economic growth.

Between 1950 and 1973, nominal GDP, that is, the growth of the size of the economic pie in Japan, was regularly growing at over 10% per year. That may not seem like a lot, but recall that that's about 4 times as fast as the average rate of growth in the United States over a similar period. For that 23-year period, Japan grows at least 4 times as fast as the U.S. We can ask ourselves, is this something that's sustainable? Is this something that's extraordinary? What is it that was a secret about Japan? Between 1965 and 1973, in this one period of time, we could look at another great episode in Japanese growth. For that short period, real growth, real buying power of individuals, grew at over 10% per year on average, nearly 11% per year. That was absolutely Japan's golden age when they seemed to break all the economic rules of gravity and defy all expectations and really leap from becoming a world leader of a kind to really being a world buster and the seeming innovator of a new economic approach that was even more successful than those that had preceded it.

Let's benchmark that number for a minute. Let's benchmark these levels of growth and think about fast in a way that really helps us feel it. If you're growing at 10% a year, you can remember this simple rule of 70 or about 72. If you divide 10% into 70, you get 7 and that means that, in Japan, average income levels were doubling about every 7 years over that period. We're talking about real buying power now. It's not just that the number of zeros or the amount of money in your bank account's going up at that rate; the real amount of material resources that you can command is doubling about every 7 years. If you live in an economy like that, you're literally going to be twice as rich in 7 years as you are today. That's remarkable; it's even hard to appreciate. At the end of 14 years, you'll be 4 times as rich. What's amazing is it's not just going to be that; it's going to be everything. It's going to be everybody. It's going to be largely true for everyone that you know. Everyone is going to get richer at about the same time.

Imagine it this way. Imagine that your kids have at least 4 times as much buying power as you did at the same point in your life as they do. In fact, they might have a little bit more if they have a little bit or even an equivalent job. They're going to live that much better, and it's happening all around you. It's almost too much to appreciate if you've never lived in an economy that grows that fast, but growth in real per capita gross domestic product—a long way to say growth in the slice of the pie that every Japanese person was able to enjoy—was growing at about 6% per year for about 40 straight years.

That actually means that the real size of economic material well-being or the resources that the Japanese population could consume grew by tenfold between 1950 and 1990. In a little more than a generation there was absolutely total transformation. If you grow your economy by 10 times, if average income levels are 10 times higher at the end of 40 years than when you began, if when you start work at 25 you're 10 times poorer than you were when you retire at 65, that's absolute transformation, and that's the miracle that was Japan at the post-war period. Japan grew so fast that even half of that rate is considered fast. That makes us ask the question and perhaps the most important question, how did they do it? How did they manage to grow at such a rate for such a long period of time? Baby, if they have a secret sauce, we need it! That's impressive, but what's the secret?

Before we explore that, and we will in some detail, let's issue a few caveats. Caveat number one was, yes, they were recovering from absolute devastation. In fact, so harsh was the war on the Japanese domestic economy that income levels in 1945 were about equivalent to income levels in 1914. In other words, because of the war, in terms of income levels they lost about 30 years of economic performance and growth. In 1940, Japan was about half as rich as the United States on this individual per capita income basis. The United States was the world leader so being half as rich wasn't necessarily bad, but it wasn't exactly at the very top of the world levels of income. After the war, Japan actually experienced a great decline in national income. That's to be expected after the devastation, but they did get back to that level. In fact, Japan returned to its pre-war level, in other words, that gap between the beginning of the war and a return to that level of growth was about 16 years. In 1956, Japan had more or less fully recovered from the devastation of the Second World War. In other words, it took them about 11 years from the end of the war in 1945 to get back to where they were at the beginning of the war. But, by 1956, Japanese income levels were only about one-third of the U.S. because the U.S. actually came out of the war really strong and grew relatively quickly. The world leader in the period of the 1950s was the United States, and Japan's income level was just about one-third of it—not rich to be sure, but it had almost fully recovered from a devastating war.

Even after they'd recovered, even after they'd got back to the levels that they had achieved prior to the war, they still grew as quickly as ever. It wasn't just a story of recovering from the devastation of the war. Japan's economic miracle extended far beyond that and remained much faster than others even after a deep economic collapse. By 1970, Japan's income levels were actually about 2/3 of the U.S. level, so file that away. In 1956, they were only about one-third of the U.S. income level, but by 1970 they were at 2/3 of the U.S. income level, so they were really catching up. Only a few years later they would reach a level that was 90–95% of the income level of many of the most advanced economies of the world, the economies of Great Britain and France.

We can think of it in a different way. By 25 years after the end of the Second World War, a war that devastated their economy, they were really back on top. They were really back at the top of world income levels and living at income levels that were only enjoyed by a select few rich nations—in fact, rich nations that had always been rich in terms of economic performance. It's an amazing story, but that's not the end. Growth after 1970 was still impressive. Despite some slowdowns because of oil embargos, Japan still grew at a much higher rate than all its peers. It grew much faster after 1970 than all the economies of Western Europe and the United States. It reached very high income levels, so high that by 1990 Japanese income levels were basically the second highest income levels in all the world. It was the second place only behind the United States, and it was a richer economy than all the Western European economies. Yes, it's true, part of the Japanese miracle was a recovery from the war, but that was only part of the story. The rest of the story is the incredible growth story that occurred after Japan had already recovered from massive devastation.

We can think about this in familiar terms, terms that we think about when we think about lots of different types of competitions. There's a story of catching up to the leader and the story that says that it's easier to catch up to the leader when you have fallen far behind. You can think about it this way: This story of economic catch-up, of a low income level economy catching up to a rich income economy, was really first described in detail by Robert Solo, who is a Nobel Prize winning economist from MIT. His story of economic growth implied that a backward nation, a nation that really was not at the forefront technologically or at an income level, could actually grow at a much faster rate than a highly developed one. You can think about it this way: If you've ever watched a cyclist going up a mountain in the Tour de France, what you know is that the cyclist at the lead who's at the point, he's at a V-formation much like geese fly in a V-formation, he's really bucking the headwind and breaking that wind for all the other riders. A rider directly behind him can have the same amount of effort, but with less effort travel even faster because they're not facing that headwind, and so it is for economic growth. The economic leaders like the United States and technological leaders like those economies of Western Europe buck the headwinds of technological advance and those behind, if they have the ability, can copy those advances and catch up much more quickly. That appears to be exactly what happened with Japan. Japan grew much faster than Europe and the United States even after they caught up to European levels of the 1970s, so a lot of that story has to be catch-up.

But, why did they catch up? Why were they able to make this leap from being backward to being at the forefront when so many other economies didn't? A lot of other economies were also backward. A lot of other economies could also copy technologies that have been proven and economic leaders in the West, but they didn't grow like the Japanese. How did they do it? Here are some of the ways that they did it.

One of the first things that they did that really broke the mold was that they had heavy cooperation between business and government. That may sound like something that is foreign to a lot of people in the West, but a real cooperation on a plan for development and growth. With plans to grow led by a government scheme to really succeed in a few key industries, the Japanese consolidated their efforts not only at the corporate level, not only at the individual level of a few plants and factories, but at a national level. In some sense, national policies were structured to grow export markets in key areas, and the Japanese knew which ones they wanted. They chose many, but in particular they chose to be successful in automobiles. They chose to be successful in steel and in electronics and in manufacturing and in manufactured goods. They created brands we know very well—Toyota, Honda, Nissan, Sony. All of these hugely successful global brands really come out of not an individual company and their plan for success, but out of cooperation between governments and firms working very closely together.

How did the governments support them? They made great loans to firms at very low interest rates. They subsidized their activities. They structured trade policies to make it easy for these firms to export to other countries while making sure that they didn't have a lot of domestic competition. In fact, that's one of the flipsides of this story. While Japan wanted to be very successful on an international basis and be very open to trade, on a domestic basis they were very closed to a lot of competition. Here again you see this full break from the idea that free markets and competition are always good. Part of the Japanese plan of cooperation was to hold these things together.

There's a second thing they did that was very important and a key to their success and ability to catch up. They had very high savings rates. When we think about savings rates, we think about personal savings rates, and that's one of them. The government can also save by running surpluses, and you can also have businesses that save by not spending all of the profits that they have. In the United States, savings rates tend to be relatively low, but in Japan they're extremely high, and this enabled them to invest in a very heavy way in their own economy.

I'll give you a little benchmark to help you understand just how high Japanese savings were. In the post-war period in the United States, personal savings rates—that's the average rate of a person's income that they save, the part they don't consume, the part they store away in the bank or under the mattress or wherever—the average rate was about 9% up until about the mid 1980s. After the mid 1980s, it went through a steep drop and actually went all the way down to zero. In Japan, savings rates were just a little bit higher. In fact, in the post-war period, Japanese savings rates averaged about 40% of income. You have to think about that. Saving on average throughout the economy very high for individuals, very high for firms, and even high for the government. A rate of 40% savings throughout this period meant that you could do things in Japan that you couldn't do in other economies. You could invest. With all that surplus of savings, you could not just buy goods, you could build roads, you could build factories. You could invest in an infrastructure that made all businesses much more successful.

One of the other consequences of a very high savings rate that may be underappreciated is that it was another way to keep the value of the yen, the currency of Japan, much lower. That high savings rate meant that Japanese were sending yen all out all over the world. They were pushing it out into other places. They saved a lot, and they needed to put that savings in places. They put it around the world, and in putting it around the world, think about putting it in the United States, they had to trade in those yen for U.S. dollars. In the process of doing that, they make the dollar more expensive and the yen less expensive. That makes them even more competitive, because if a yen is expensive to a person who owns a dollar, then Japanese exports are less expensive to a person who owns a dollar. That helps reinforce this system of cooperation between government and business.

They also had more than that, but a lot of the savings they invested not just in things and in infrastructure, but in people. They had very deep investments in education that reinforced this drive to be technologically more sophisticated, that enabled them to compete on a level that they couldn't compete on before, really head to head not just in productivity, but in the intellectual conquests that are required in modern business.

In the process throughout all of this, they had, for the most part, great political stability. Stability, however it's achieved, actually is a good thing. It's not always a super good thing, it's not a good thing if it comes at very high costs, but in economic terms you do have that gut feeling to say stability is very good for the economy because with stability comes an incentive to invest. If the future's predictable, even if it's not one that you perfectly favor over all other outcomes, you have a little more incentive to invest because you understand the costs and benefits better. Humans are much more likely to make long-term investments and to take risks when the stable outcomes for the future are more knowable. That doesn't mean that they're democratic, but they were in Japan. They did have a democracy, yes, and a very stable one. They also increased the ability to pour lots of funds into long-term investments. With political stability comes the ability to execute much longer-term plans.

In some sense, Japan is the prototypical example of a state-led government economy, but it's not the only example of the successes of state-led growth. History has, of course, presented many of them to us. We could look at South Korea. We could certainly look at China of course and understand that these heavily involved governments have not always produced the failures we might associate with government involvement in a largely free market and open economy. But, do we largely and typically acknowledge this fact that some state-led approaches have been largely successful? Even command economies, ones that seem to engage in all manner of control over what's produced, for whom it's produced, and what prices are charged, do seem to grow faster in some ways than free market ones. In some ways, that butts up against the strong story I've been telling you about incentives being sharp and the free market being golden and working its magic. In fact it does and in fact it has, but maybe there's something we don't understand if in fact a command economy can also grow as fast as a free market one. What's the lesson we can begin to take away from this? What unites this potential divide?

There's one thing that's certainly true—if the story's about economic growth, and that's what we want to understand, then it's really simple. Growth is really all about economic productivity, full stop. That's it. If you achieve productivity growth, which is the ability to take resources and extract more value from them over time, if you can continue that process, in some ways it doesn't matter how you get there as long as you get there. As I had mentioned before, there seemed to be more than one path. If there's an organizing framework that we might use to think about this that really unites command economy approaches and free-market economy approaches, it's a difficult one, but I have an idea for you. If we divide all economic activity into just about 3 buckets, we can begin to understand where productivity comes from and how it relates to all sorts of government approaches. If we understand where productivity comes from, we understand how policies, even very different policies, seem to work to produce economic growth and raise material living standards. Let's think about 3 basic buckets that relate to the overall productivity of an economy.

First of all, we can think about productivity in the following sense: When we talk about productivity, we're imagining total production. Imagine any factory as a shorthand for the overall economy and think how do we make the most production out of this given set of resources—out of the land, labor, technology, and human beings there? There are a couple of keys and in the economic sense there are at least 3 distinct buckets.

The first bucket we might think of is a bucket that we think of when we think about demographics. That's what we might call a labor force bucket. We might think about demographics being the proportion of the labor force relative to the overall economy. If we're really worried about the size of the slices, and we're really worried about how much output we have per person, then the first thing we need is a lot of output and few people. If you have a lot of output and few people, you have a lot of output per person. How do you get that? One way is to have a very high and large labor force relative to the total population. In other words, you want to have a high fraction of your economy filled with people between the ages of about 16 and 70, people at the prime of their working age. This is because people that are younger than about 16 and people that are older than about 70, we love them, but they're really not usually very economically productive. They're not producing economic output; they're really only consuming economic output. One term that helps is that demographic term. In Japan, they actually had very favorable demographics, a distribution of the population where after the Second World War a very large proportion of the population was between the ages of 16 and 70. Fewer young people and fewer old people lead to a greater economic output per person.

The second thing that we can think of is to have a high employment level. It's great if you have a lot of people who are able to work, but it's really important that they have a job to go to. Even if you have favorable demographics, but you don't have jobs, you don't get a lot of production. The second bucket we can think of is the employment bucket. Having a lot of people that are actually with jobs and employed is critical. One of the key forces in economic success is having a macro economy that produces lots of jobs. That's why an economy like the U.S. with a low unemployment rate is more productive and richer than most of its peers. The same is true in Japan. In Japan, unemployment rates are as low as 2% and that's because they have a very successful macroeconomic management plan and a social infrastructure that supports jobs and keeping people employed.

If we think about those 2 terms, the demographic term and the employment term, we account for a lot of the differences in growth across countries. It's about one-third of the story, but 2/3 of the story is actually something else, and that's left to the most important bucket we have. If there's one bucket that really explains most of the differences in economic performance and most of the differences whether it's a free-market economy or whether it's a state-led economy, it's just something we call average worker productivity. It's the most important bucket. It explains about 2/3 of all the differences between rich and poor countries—it's the big enchilada. It's everything. If you're a productive economy, and if you have high average worker productivity, you're a rich economy. They're really one and the same thing, but what is average worker productivity? It's a really simple ratio. It's just the ratio of total economic output, which is gross domestic product, divided by the employed workers. The average worker productivity is the average amount of economic output produced by active workers in your economy. In rich economies, it's high, and in poor economies, it's low, and there really are no exceptions to that rule.

What matters too about this definition is it's not just productivity in the Sonys and it's not just productivity in the Toyotas or the General Electrics or the Disneys or the Apples, it's productivity across the entire economy. It's the average worker productivity for every job. Every worker matters in an economy, every worker represents a resource, and it doesn't matter if you have one firm that's lights out, super terrific, really a high performer and the other 99% of your economy is filled with workers who aren't very productive or who work in inefficient firms. Average worker productivity is the key to economic success, and it's the key variable, the key bucket that unites state-led approaches that are successful and free-market approaches that are successful.

Then we ask another question. If the real key to productivity, if most of it is having high average worker productivity, what makes workers more productive? There are a couple of things that come immediately to mind, and they're really important. There's training. More educated workers that are trained to do their jobs and can execute on the jobs well tend to be more productive. They make fewer mistakes, they make better decisions, and they tend to execute better and create higher value products and services. Training matters a lot, but training isn't free. You have to have an economy that invests in people and helps make them better. In the same way, things that aren't related to workers can make them more productive, like a good infrastructure. Efficient roads, efficient ports, efficient electrical systems, and broadband Internet, all of these things help make workers more productive, because they make it easier for them to do their jobs and they lower the cost of delivering products to market. These things are also not free, and you need an economy that can invest in infrastructure to help make highly trained workers more productive.

There's another thing you can do. It's not really about efficiency; it's just about effort. You can be more productive in the sense of having higher output by simply working more hours. In Japan, workers worked a lot of hours. They worked more throughout this post-war period than most of their counterparts around the world, including the United States. It wasn't just that they were being trained more, that they had a better infrastructure year in and year out. They were also working harder, and all of these things make workers more productive. When you have more productive workers on average, you have more economic growth and more economic success, and that's part of the Japanese miracle.

You need even more than that. You need a lot of things in fact, but one of them is you have to have products and services that people want to buy and that people are willing to buy in largely free global markets. That's another thing that Japan did well. They had the ability to sell year in and year out more expensive products. They began producing rather simple things and year in and year you graduated to higher value-added products. These higher value-added products returned to make worker productivity higher because the more bang for the buck, the more revenue per hour of work, the higher is average worker productivity. It's these investments of human time and effort into the personal skills in an environment that rewards those personal skills and helps them become more productive that really separates rich economies from poor economies.

That requires even more. It's a complex story, but an investment in skill requires lots of confidence. It requires confidence in the people to make investments and to take those risks. In the free-market approach, we see confidence generated because there are rags-to-riches stories. There's evidence over time of people whose entrepreneurial activity, whose hard efforts, whose deep investments into their own talents and deep investments into new products and services, pay off. In the Japanese style economy, there's confidence because there's political stability, and there's evidence of success. There are those years when growth is everywhere to be seen and it's 10% per year, year in and year out. After a while, you've been shown that this system works, and you're confident, and so you invest. Even if you don't have confidence, maybe the government has a substitute for confidence. One of the best substitutes for confidence is just to make the investments yourself. That doesn't always work, but in some cases a government can make investments in infrastructure and in business to substitute for the confidence that a free-market economy might need to make those same investments. In Japan, we see a lot of this.

Maybe the big takeaway is that high investments funded by high savings, generated and supported by an economy with lots of political stability, and a workforce that's growing in skill gets you to more productive people throughout the economy. It gets you to much higher average worker productivity, even if you didn't get there with the same free-market approach. That's hard to sustain. There's no silver bullet answer to the problem of how to sustain this and how to make that work over time, but that's largely the story of the Japanese miracle that began at the end of the Second World War and carried all the way through to 1990.

In closing we might ask was that a representation of a successful economy? The Japanese economy grew at faster speeds than ever seen before, it caught up to the world leaders, and in some sense it's the most successful economy of the 20th century. Is that the whole story? In some sense, it isn't, because it's not the end of the story because after that 40 years of growth from 1950–1990, Japan, like the United States before it, entered into its own great depression. It entered into a period where it lost a lot of ground and the basis for this story, this unifying story that led to high worker productivity, really fell in on itself. We'll revisit this story in later lectures and think about what it is that made this example fail just as a fully free-market approach had failed before it.

The good part is that Japan is largely back on track, and it has to some degree regained a lot of its stability that it lost in the period of the 1990s to at least the year 2000. But, the failure of this economy, the most successful in the last half of the 20th century, matched up with the story of the Great Depression and the failures of Western economies and the free-market approach, forces us to ask a lot more questions about economic growth. It's true there seem to be many paths to economic success, and by the same token, there are many failures that lay and wait for all economic approaches, or so it seems.

# The Secrets of Rapid Growth in Tiger Economies
## Lecture 8

These are miracles of a different kind. They're not like the Japanese and the U.S. and the Western European miracles. These are miracles of a more recent vintage, miracles of poor countries and small countries, countries that one might think the world could easily overlook, but didn't, and they made it happen.

So far, we've looked at the growth of countries that were already relatively rich when they began to grow. In this lecture, we turn to our first examples of low-income countries that experienced the kind of economic growth we associate with the modern era. This is the story of the Asian Tigers: Hong Kong, Taiwan, Singapore, and South Korea.

These economies are studied together for a number of reasons: They all experienced amazing growth at about the same time. They were all Asian and had somewhat similar cultural roots. And in all these countries, the workers had an extraordinary work ethic and great trust in their leadership. If we look carefully at the Asian Tigers, however, we find some significant differences—in culture, history, geography, and economic strategy. Hong Kong, for example, probably had the most economic freedom of any country in the world, while Singapore might be the ultimate exemplar of government control; nonetheless, the two experienced remarkable growth during the same period.

If the differences were large and the similarities weren't all that apparent, what was the secret of the Asian Tigers? We can find the answer by working backwards. We know, for example, that the secret to economic growth is increasing average worker productivity. Whatever the Tigers were doing, they were making their average workers more productive. They did this with very high savings rates at the national level, stable and relatively low wages over a long period of time, and political stability.

High savings rates are important because they enable investments in infrastructure and education. The Tigers had both high savings rates and high investment rates, which they funded themselves. At the same time, they kept wages low so that they could pass along their increased productivity at low prices to consumers around the world. The Tigers also managed to sustain political stability and generate some level of confidence among the people, no mean feat in a poor economy.

It's difficult to identify anything other than these three general factors that led to growth, but they seem to be enough to teach us a few lessons about how growth can be generated in a poor economy. As we saw with Japan, starting out poor can itself be an advantage. Our three buckets also give us a partial explanation for the Tigers' economic success. Most of the Tigers had a high labor force relative to the population, which results in rapid growth in per capita GDP. The Tigers also had low unemployment rates, which generated buy-in from the people and laid the groundwork for political stability.

> **In that short period of time, [the Asian Tigers] really became a big part of the workshop of the world. They weren't just regional players expanding locally; they were expanding globally.**

The Tigers remain in extraordinarily good positions, and they represent a different kind of economic miracle—miracles of small, poor countries coming to the economic fore. They teach us that there is no single culture or strategy that is perfectly adapted to growth. They also teach us that a mix of some free-market activity and some government control may be a wise approach. Finally, they show us that the Industrial Revolution wasn't just a feature of Western European economies. It could be spread about, democratized to the rest of the world, but doing so isn't easy, and the experience of the Asian Tigers raises questions about why their miracles can't be replicated elsewhere. ∎

## Suggested Reading

Rajan and Zingales, *Saving Capitalism from the Capitalists*.
Yergin and Stanislaw, *The Commanding Heights*.

Lecture 8: The Secrets of Rapid Growth in Tiger Economies

1. Can the success of Asian Tiger economies be attributed to common policies or cultural characteristics?

2. How important to the world economy are the Asian Tigers? Can poorer countries in Africa and Latin America follow the same course as these economies? Why or why not?

# The Secrets of Rapid Growth in Tiger Economies
## Lecture 8—Transcript

Welcome back. In previous lectures, we paid an awful lot of attention to economic miracles. We studied the first miracle, if you will, the miracle of the birth of modern economic growth that occurred in England and the rest of Western Europe. We studied that miracle for all the lessons it gives us to understand all subsequent periods of economic growth, and it has a lot of lessons to share. We also studied the United States and its miraculous ascent from a developing economy of its own to being the world's largest economy at the beginning and throughout all of the 20th century. We also studied the economic miracle of Japan, the speed record holder for economic growth in the 20th century. The Japanese miracle is one of the most profound and interesting periods of economic development and growth in all of economic history.

These miracles teach us a lot about the fundamentals of growth and what it takes to grow. But, they all actually have something in common that is kind of a conundrum. They were actually already relatively rich countries when they begin to grow. You might even say that we've only studied miracles in countries that were already pretty well off. For the most part, the biggest stories of economic development and growth very late into the 20th century didn't include any truly poor countries. It was all about who was already strong, who was already on top, who was already rich, and that's kind of a flaw for us. To really understand growth, maybe we should also understand what it looks like from the very poorest vantage point.

In this lecture, what we'd like to do is discuss the first real examples of truly low income or poor countries that began to grow rich and began to have economic growth like that we associate with the modern era. To understand this, we can look at some of the first countries, the ones that really initiated this idea, the belief that to really be rich you didn't have to start rich. To really be powerful, you didn't have to start powerful. You could go from humble to wonderful in a generation, and that's the story of the Asian Tigers.

That name might be familiar, but if we think about the Asian Tigers, a few countries come to mind. We think about Hong Kong, which is really a special administrative zone of China, Taiwan, Singapore, and South Korea. Beginning in about the late 1960s and a little bit earlier in some cases, these economies did something miraculous. All the while during this period, if you'll recall, Japan was growing really rapidly and scaring a lot of the leaders in the First World club that they were going to be caught up and surpassed. At that same time, the Asian Tigers were catching up on Japan. The numbers are really astounding when you think about them. From 1960 to the year 2000, a period of only about 40 years, the Asian Tigers went from having income levels of their people that were about one-third of Japanese levels or in some cases only one-fifth of Japanese levels to being nearly equivalent a generation later. That's no easy trick. After all, we know that Japan wasn't exactly sitting still during this period. Whatever there was to a secret of economic growth and going from poor to rich, the Tigers seemed to have that secret.

This was actually really big. This is what I would call an "aha moment" in the study of economic growth in history. It was a moment where we could say, hey, wait a minute something's happening. In these countries that appear to be proximate or some way similar, but they're doing what we previously thought might be impossible, which was to grow at a rate like Japan was growing and to do it year in and year out, 30–40 years in a row. It was an extraordinary period when we'd looked at those economies and asked what's so right about them? What's so wrong about us or about everyone else? In that short period of time, those 4 economies really became a big part of the workshop of the world. They weren't just regional players expanding locally; they were expanding globally. Turn over any item in your house, a toaster or a television, a plastic vase, and it probably said made in Hong Kong or South Korea or some such. This was a period of magic, and that magic occurred in the Tigers, and it's for that reason that we study them.

Some things come to mind. We do group them together and there are good reasons for that. One, they were all growing about the same time at about the same amazing rate, but there were other similarities, or at least what were apparent similarities that seem to stand out. There was this Asian idea. All of these economies were in Asia. They seemed to have some similar cultural roots, although that was probably much of an overstatement. When you examine the activities in those economies, when you went to the factory floors, talk to the people, they seem to have an amazing will, an extraordinary work ethic. They were winning, but they were working hard to win, and it was obvious. They also seemed to have a great trust in leadership, or at least more trust in their leaders than maybe other economies in the West had in their own. For this reason, a lot of observers from around the world began to look at the Asian Tigers as sort of a standing lesson to the rest of the world. For about the same period of time, a lot of the old winners, the old lion rich economies in the West, were really slowing down. They were becoming a little more dull. They were losing their edge. To many, losing this edge to these vibrant economies with trust in leadership and amazing will seem to be sort of an atonement for our own loss of unity and our own loss of work ethic. There was a sense in which we were just being out-competed and the Asian Tigers knew how to out-compete us.

There was also a belief that there must have been some idea, some common policy, some common set of plan or secret that they shared that enabled them to grow at this super ordinary rate. After all, could it be possible that this was just coincidence, that these 4 economies somewhat near one another in somewhat similar cultures would all start to grow at amazing rates at the same time? It just seemed too uncommon to be true.

In fact, the truth was not so black and white. Once you looked really carefully at the Asian Tigers, you did notice that they grew at about the same rate, but there were actually some very significant differences. Not just significance in the culture and the history and geography, there are differences in their economic strategy. If what they were doing economically was the key, then they were doing very different things. In some sense, their success evidenced what we've already known, that there seem to be more than one path to economic growth.

I'll give you a simple example. Think about 2 of the Tigers and the contrast between them. Think about Hong Kong versus Singapore. If you look on any economic map of freedom around the world or the place where the government is the least involved in business and places the least restrictions on business in any modern economy, Hong Kong probably rates number one—the most free economy and perhaps the best example of a classical economic free-market model. Producers aren't told what to produce, how much to produce, and what to charge. They're allowed to do what they want. This has been part of Hong Kong's culture for many years. It's a trading spot. It's always been this hub of great activity and it's very free. The rules, well, there don't seem to be many rules at all in Hong Kong, and that's part of their secret, but they were growing crazy fast.

In contrast, think about Singapore. Singapore is this tiny remote fishing village truly insignificant to the world by about 1950. There was really nothing there. It had a geographic spot that made it approximate to a lot of important shipping lanes, but otherwise not much. They grew at about the same rate, but they might be the ultimate example of control. We think about their leader Lee Kuan Yew and all the decisions that he made. They didn't just make decisions about what to produce; they made decisions about strategy 5 years in advance. This was a team approach. They were calling plays all the way up in the press box at the president's office, and that's the way that Singapore had its growth. It's very different from Hong Kong, very much a controlled market economy. The similarities, if it were true, you couldn't see it in a lot of the things the Tigers did, at least not from the vantage point of clear economic strategy. This wasn't a free markets versus mixed approach or free markets versus state approach; it was a mix of a lot of things in between.

Even if we look at an economy like South Korea, it was different than Hong Kong and Singapore, not quite as strict as Singapore with regard to its planning and certainly not as free with regard to its rules and trade as Hong Kong. If we say anything about [South Korea] it's that it was probably the most like Japan. It had plans; it had strong cooperation between business and governments. Banks worked very closely with firms that they loaned to. They also seemed to have a lot of cultural buy-in, a lot of belief in the system and the way it worked. As a result, they had extraordinary growth. But, they're not really culturally the same as a lot of these other places. The apparent similarities weren't really all that apparent the closer you looked, neither in economic strategy nor perhaps in other characteristics as well.

Then there's Taiwan. Taiwan is this real interesting example of an economy that has all the characteristics of its neighbor China. Yet it was growing at extraordinary rates, even while China was stagnating and not growing at all.

It was a real hodgepodge of policies and over a 40-year period in any country you'll see a hodgepodge of polices, but that's what you saw in Taiwan. It was a big mix, and they really became the workshop of the world. If anything, Taiwan was the leader in the field of becoming the workshop of the world and climbing the value chain from lower value-added products to higher value-added products. What the Taiwanese taught us is what the Tigers knew or didn't know, but what the worst of the world would try to emulate for many years later.

What was it then? If the differences were large and the similarities weren't all that apparent, what was the secret? Was it culture? It didn't seem like it. Was it geography? They were all in Asia, but it's a big place. It doesn't seem like geography. Was it economic strategy? I don't see how that could be true. The strategies were just too different. They didn't have one strategy. There wasn't a tiger policy. There were lots of tiger policies. The thing is they were all working. So what was it?

Maybe this doesn't help us as much as we thought, but there had to be something there and certainly there was. It wasn't exactly coincidence. They weren't all growing at the same rate at the same time just because. It wasn't just that it was the right time and they all got lucky. There were some things, and we can examine those things. It's hard to understand, but we can actually get to the answer by sort of working backwards. For example, we know that the secret to economic growth at the end of the day is making your average workers more productive year in and year out. Whatever the Tigers were doing, they were making their average workers much more and more productive. We can then begin to ask, how do you do that, and how did they do that? There were a couple of things that they all seemed to do that really ran against all the differences and seemed to make all the difference in the secret of growth for the Tigers.

There were 3 big things, and we should spend some time going into some detail on them. In my view, the 3 big things were very high savings rates at the national level, not just personal, but the national level. The second big thing I think was stable and relatively low wages over a long period of time. The last one is really something you almost always have to have or it certainly seems to, and that's political stability. In all of these examples you did have political stability. You had economies that were run differently in different ways by different people and by different leaders over this period, but there was sufficient stability and sufficient fluidity in the policies that it seemed to have been enough to generate confidence.

Let's spend some time on that first one, a high savings rate because it's something we see over and over in the stories of successful growth economies. Savings seems to be something that's good in and of itself. Don't good people save money? Isn't it good for a person to save and for a country to save and not run deficits? That moralistic line of reasoning has some sway, but it's really not the reason that economists think about savings as important. Savings is important because it's really a means to an end. It's one very stable and reasonable means to the end of making investments. When I say investments I don't mean buying stocks in this company or that or bonds; I mean real investments in hard things, plant property and equipment, infrastructure, roads, airports, ports, broadband infrastructure. We think about investing in education and in people skills, and those are the things that make you more productive. That's what makes an economy more productive year in and year out. Without investments to replace the things that depreciate, to up your skills and stay up with the competition, any economy will stagnate.

What the Tigers all did is they had very high savings rates, and that meant that they could also have very high investment rates, investments that they themselves funded. They didn't have to go begging around the world paying high interest rates or worrying that all those other economies that invested in them would pull out. They saved for themselves, and that's not hard to do. In saving upwards of 30–40% of gross domestic product per year, the Tigers embarked upon a plan of huge investments that really transformed the economy. Massive increases in productivity of labor generally come from big increases in investment.

They also had relatively low wages, so think about those 2 things together. It wasn't just that they were growing more productive year in and year out expanding the infrastructure to help their workers become more productive to make the bang for the buck of productivity all the much more higher, they were also keeping their wages low. That meant that they could pass along a lot more productivity at low prices to consumers around the world. That's not easy to do. To keep the wages low meant they had to engage in macroeconomic policies that kept their currencies relatively cheap and to sort of sustain political support even while those people who were really delivering the goods of making the economy richer were not receiving such high wages. But, it was seen as part of the plan, and it's something that really worked. It wasn't just cheap goods for a rich West in Japan, although that was part of it, it was holding together this economy in this particular way.

What the Tigers also did in addition to having high savings, in addition to having relatively low wages, is that they had stability, and we know that this matters. You have to have buy-in to the plan. You need the security in order to make those investments. Investments mean putting money aside that you could use today to consume. If you're a poor economy, that's not an easy thing to do. Can you really convince someone who's relatively low income to save everything? Trust me, in 10 years, it's all going to work out. That's not easy, but this is what they were able to manufacture, some buy-in to the plan. To manufacture in sometimes good ways and sometimes not so good ways the security and stability needed to change people's behavior in order to generate economic growth.

That sounds like 3 relatively small things, and I'm sure there's more to the story, but it gets a little more complex after that. These are 3 we can really hang our hats on. If there's anything else, it's really hard to tell. When you have a story like this, and you can pin it down a little bit and say, the Asian Tigers were really different, they didn't have one plan but many, and the commonalities of the plan seemed to be things like buy-in and high savings and political stability, you might ask how did they get those things? If those things are the secrets and that's what really works, let's pass it along. Let's get others to do it. Or, maybe we could ask why didn't they do it years before? Certainly they wanted the growth before, right? What's the story? What's the cause of those causes and maybe what's the cause of the cause of the causes? That's an inherently difficult thing to answer in almost any scientific pursuit, but especially in a field like economics.

It always reminds me of this cute Greek story I remember of these 2 soldiers overlooking the Mediterranean. As they're looking out over the sea and pondering things, one of them says, what holds up the earth? The other soldier said, that's easy, Atlas holds up the earth. The first soldier's kind of satisfied for a minute and then he said, wait a minute, what is Atlas standing on? The second soldier said, that's easy, too, he's standing on a turtle. The second soldier's satisfied for a minute and says, what's the turtle on? The other soldier says he's on another turtle. Before the next words can get out, that one soldier says, friend, don't ask any more questions—it's turtles all the way down, which is another way of saying the root cause of the root cause of the root cause is almost impossible for a lot of us to discern for a lot of reasons. Certainly in this case it is hard. It's hard to hang your hat on much more than these somewhat general issues that seem to have led to growth, but that's what we have and that seems to be enough to teach us a few lessons about how growth can be generated even in a really poor economy.

In fact, starting poor might actually be part of the reason that things work out well. We recall this from the lecture on Japan when we said just like a cyclist who's at the back of the pack, who can sort of draft up on the leader because the wind is being made a lot easier and being structured away from the headwind, in that sense starting poor can be kind of an advantage. But, it also has some disadvantages. As I mentioned before, to be poor means that it's really hard to encourage somebody to really save. The poor are often very much concerned about their future, and they want to be very cautious, but it also means giving up a lot at the wrong time. Exactly when things are getting a little bit better, you still need to save a lot for that rainy day. Exactly when the government could be a little more generous and when firms can be a little more generous with wages, they weren't. There was that discipline that seemed to matter a lot. The advantages and disadvantages of starting poor was something that the Tigers seemed to manage pretty well.

Perhaps it was a lucky break that led them to be able to do this, but it doesn't really seem to be true. It seems to be much more than that. That takes us back perhaps to this idea of productivity. We can ask ourselves what is it that really made the Tigers as successful as they were? If we think about the 3 buckets that we talked about in previous lectures, we said you could be lucky with productivity and the fact that you could have a very high labor force relative to the population. In other words, if virtually everybody was of working age, then everybody's out there making economic product, and there's nobody who's just consuming the product. In that sense, the slices of economic pie, the per capita GDP, grow really quickly. Was this true of the Tigers? In fact, for most of them it actually was. They had relatively few people who were beyond working age and comparatively few people who were actually below working age as well. During this period of time of really high growth, they actually did extraordinarily well. They actually had favorable demographics. It's a small contribution to what otherwise was a terrific story.

What about the second big bucket? Remember, it's not just that you have an active labor force and a large proportion of your population of working age—you've got to have jobs for them. If they don't have jobs, they're not producing economic output. How did they do that on that score? Actually, they did really well. On the score of creating low unemployment, one of the basic metrics for any successful economy, the Tigers did great. They had very low unemployment rates. They were creating lots of jobs and these things began to work together. Because they were successful early enough to create jobs for people, they generated more buy-in. In generating more buy-in, they lay the groundwork for more political stability to come. All of these things seemed to work together and worked very well together. It's an extraordinary story of how some economies just seem to mix things well together when a lot of other economies didn't. That makes us ask other questions. If the Tigers could do it, why can't everybody? If the Tigers did it, was it something that was sustainable? We can answer that by asking where are they now? If we think of the Tigers and where are they now, we say, they're extraordinarily good. Not only did they go from poor to rich in 40 years, but they really have stayed that way, so it wasn't just a transitory event.

These are miracles of a different kind. They're not like the Japanese and the U.S. and the Western European miracle. These are miracles of a more recent vintage, miracles of poor countries and small countries, countries that one might think the world could easily overlook, but didn't, and they made it happen. The great leader of Singapore Lee Kuan Yew once said his entire strategy was simple. I just want to make Singapore relevant to the world, because why else would this tiny little village perhaps be relevant? He made it so through their plans and their activities and all the things they did to make themselves so productive. It's a great story and an inspiring one. It reminds us that miracles like those, full transformations of poor economies to rich ones, transformations of lives from people with very humble beginnings who don't have much could live much better, and their children could live even better. It exists. We have the examples; therefore, it must be possible.

We would think it must be possible in other countries as well, but why is it so elusive? Why is it so hard to copy that particular strategy? We seem to have the game plan right in front of us when we look at the U.S., perhaps, or Japan, or the Western economies that succeeded at the beginning of the Industrial Revolution. But, it seems so hard to copy. More recently we have the Tigers, countries and economies that didn't have everything going for them but seemed to make it work anyway. Why is it so elusive? Why is it so hard to get?

One of the reasons is that perhaps we look at things from a simple vantage point. We expect there to be a single strategy or one culture that's perfectly adapted to growth. But, most of the evidence we have in economic history tells us there's just not a single strategy for growth. There's not one culture that works so much better than the others that it's truly impossible for one culture to grow. Some may argue that, but the evidence doesn't really support that idea. We see a broad range of strategies and a relatively broad range of cultures have at least some success for a reasonable period of time. That makes understanding the secrets to growth and how to pass it on to countries that don't have it all the more difficult.

One of the things that we do see in the Tigers that we can carry forward would be that they did have a mix of government control over the economy and some free-market activity. Really if you don't think about Hong Kong, which pursued the most pure free-market approach, all the other economies did have a relatively active government. I think there are a lot of problems with a really active government, and I would be wary of any government that thought it could just manufacture growth through its own strategy. But, these are examples where some of these approaches seemed to be really successful. Certainly that's appealing to a lot of political leaders.

We may ask can anyone do that? Can any country actually go out and copy what these economies did? It's not easy to tell, and certainly what we have seen is that the miracle of the Asian economies has been very hard to transmit. Very shortly after the success of these economies became very apparent, we saw lots of copycats. We saw lots of economies through Latin America, Eastern Europe, and Africa try the same approaches. Most of them actually didn't succeed. We've explored these miracles for the lessons that they can teach us about the eradication of poverty through growth, but we haven't really discovered how to make them "copyable." We haven't really discovered how to take those examples and replicate them in a consistent way in a different geography with different leaders in a different culture. It seems frustrating, but we can take what we know from the lessons and keep trying, keep repeating experiments until we get things right.

What the Asian Tigers teach us is that this idea that some of us might call the American dream of rags to riches, of starting humbly and poor and in short sleeves, and then becoming wealthier and having children who live very well, that American dream has been repeated. In single generations, countries have gone from poor to rich around the world. In some sense, what the Tigers show us is that the Industrial Revolution wasn't just a feature of Western European economies. It could be spread about, democratized to the rest of the world, but it's not easy. I mean, think about it. If growth were easy, everyone would have it. If growth were easy, then we wouldn't live in the world we live in today where we have differentials that are extraordinarily high in per capita income.

Think about this for a moment—there are a number of countries in the world, many countries in the world in fact, where the vast majority of the population lives on about $1 per day. There are lots of countries in the world where people live on $100 per day. At a difference of about 100 to 1, something's got to be wrong. Something about spreading these ideas must be difficult. There must be more that we don't understand. Growth is not easy and that's the reason that everybody doesn't have it. That's really our homework. That's what we take away from these examples. They're lessons. What they can teach us about productivity, which is primary, what they can teach us about stability and coordination of a plan, the value of having discipline and high savings rates, and then they can teach us to ask better questions. Why isn't that enough? Why can't we simply copy those conditions and spread them about? It's not that easy and that's the homework that we all have.

We might say in closing that the miracle of the Asian Tigers is something that answered a lot of questions and raised even more. But, the questions that it did answer really helped us think about enduring problems of understanding the secrets of growth. For one, it doesn't seem to be that the Tigers followed an ideology per se. They didn't seem to follow an ism. Maybe they believed that they did. Maybe in their heart of hearts the plan was so compelling, maybe in their heart of hearts, the idea seemed to be so true, that they just closed their ideas and believed that they had one of these plans. Maybe that was enough. Maybe that's even the function of these ideologies and isms. But, it's not. It's something beyond that. That's one of the reasons why it's so hard to copy. It's so hard to change economies that are poor into economies that are rich. Mercifully we can look back at the examples that these economies give us. We can look at what they taught us and the miracles that they produced in the 40 years from 1960 to the year 2000. We can say, terrific. We have a wonderful example of how things can be done. It exists; it must be possible. Mercifully, that's true for the Asian Tigers. They went from poor to rich in a generation, and they've stayed that way ever since.

# Lessons and Limits of Japan's Economic Model
## Lecture 9

**... [N]o one really knows what the economic models of Japan will look like in the future or whether or not they'll teach us that, in fact, they are less vulnerable to some of the other ills that befall other strategies and other economies. Perhaps it's a lesson that all glory passes and that no economy, no leader, is ever invulnerable.**

As we've seen, the Japanese economy was one of the most successful ever, but it went from the stuff of legend to a cautionary tale in a very short period of time. In the 1970s, it seemed that Western economic models were stagnating. The U.S. economy at the time was lackluster, with relatively high inflation and high unemployment. The world was primed to believe in a new model of growth, and Japan provided it. By the 1980s, the lessons of Japanese success were being taught in business schools around the world.

During Japan's 40 years of spectacular growth, low interest rates had driven an extraordinary degree of investment in land, resulting in a huge surge in property values. Then, around 1990, this property bubble began to wobble and, eventually, burst. The secret to bubbles growing large and being very difficult to live in when they shrink is **leverage**—the degree to which an investor uses borrowed money. Through the use of leverage, corporations and investors in Japan drove the Nikkei Index to a high of about 40,000. Then, the economic miracle of Japan came to an abrupt stop. Most hoped the resulting recession would pass quickly, but it didn't.

Whenever an economy is recovering from a huge asset decline, such as a property bubble bursting, the resulting **deflation** is extremely difficult to overcome. In Japan, property values fell so far and so fast that the thin margin of leverage protecting investors began to erode rapidly, and they couldn't pay off their debts. The scramble to sell property then added fuel to the fire of deflation. In this situation, property values fall, people panic and cut prices in an attempt to sell, and others wait to buy because prices are falling.

One of the first casualties in any property bubble is the banks, which supplied the money to pay for the property to begin with. In Japan, the banks realized that the values they had loaned to were way off, and with no way to recoup their losses quickly, they faced collapse. The Japanese government stepped in in a big way, injecting substantial amounts of money into the banking system and the economy (monetary easing) and engaging in massive expenditures.

Did the strategy of the Japanese government work? The short answer is no. Japan experienced more than a decade of economic loss. The country went massively into debt without government spending really making a difference. We can draw a few simple lessons from the Japanese experience: First, the government waited too long to rescue the banks. It also seems true that the dynamism that motivated Japan for so long was a necessary component to its success and has never really been regained. Further, bubbles are deadly; letting asset values rise beyond what seems reasonable will topple any economy. Finally, deflation is absolutely paralyzing. Despite its fall from grace, Japan is still a rich country. But the experience of Japan showed the world that its model was just as vulnerable to economic ills as any other. ■

> … [T]he miracle of Japan really came to a full, complete, and abrupt stop. Suddenly, everything seemed to be going wrong. It wasn't just a hiccup. The Nikkei began to plummet and plummet quickly. Property values began to plummet and plummet quickly. … That economy and that miracle absolutely seemed to be over.

## Important Terms

**deflation**: A situation of falling prices for goods and services.

**leverage**: The use of credit to enhance an investor's ability to make additional investments.

## Suggested Reading

Bastiat, *Economic Fallacies*.

Friedman and Schwartz, *A Monetary History of the United States*.

Keynes, *The General Theory of Employment, Interest and Money*.

Krugman, *The Return of Depression Economics*.

## Questions to Consider

1. What were the principal causes of Japan's lost decade of economic growth? Were they predictable?

2. What lessons do we learn about economic growth from Japan's meteoric rise and precipitous fall?

# Lessons and Limits of Japan's Economic Model
## Lecture 9—Transcript

Welcome back. Through the early lectures of this course we've examined lots of economic miracles. This makes a lot of sense if you think about it as I argued earlier. What we want to do is to uncover some of the secrets of successful economies and of rapid economic growth. It makes a lot of sense, therefore, to look at the most successful economies. We had to talk a little bit about what makes an economy successful, then identify the winners, and look into their stories.

This is a very sensible thing to do in any field of endeavor. If you want to understand how to be a superstar athlete, you should probably study some of the superstar athletes. If you want to know how to be a great surgeon or the like, study the best in the field. But, in some sense, that's only part of the story because understanding how one gets successful may not unravel and uncover all the secrets of growth. We also need to look at some of those economies that tried, but failed, or that succeeded and then failed. In that sense, we ought to turn our attention a little bit to some grand economic failures. It's time to do that and consider what we can learn by considering a big failure of sorts, a real genuine fall from grace. The surprise is we've already studied that economy.

The Japanese economy was one of the most successful ever. You can look through all the records, you can study all the charts, and you're going to be really hard pressed to find any economy that performed better than Japan. I think the real shocker is that as extraordinarily successful as Japan was, as super important was the story of Japan's rise from 1950–90, in a very short period of time, that economy went from a legendary economy, one that would break all the rules and lead the pack, to a cautionary tale. It happened very, very quickly.

It's hard to overstate just how big the celebration was about Japan's growth, the hyperbole surrounding their success was extraordinary, and it really swept the world. One place you could see this were in all the top business schools around the world. Business schools were certain—and I don't mean a little true or somewhat confident—they were certain about what caused the success of Japan's economy, of what caused the great rise of its huge corporations. In short and to exaggerate a bit, what was the cause was everything about Japan. It seemed that they were so good, everything they did was right. It was the way that they lived, the way that they talked, the way they communicated. It was the structure of cooperation in their business and not competition amongst their businesses. It was having a government that was actively involved, not one that stepped back and said let's let businesses do what businesses want to do.

As a result, we saw a huge flood of books and terrific lessons about what the Japanese were doing and what they did right. Experts from all corners and all fields looked at Japan's models, they looked at the way they ran businesses, ran governments, ran societies, ran schools, ran families, and said this is all that we need to do. The better way has been shown. It's the Japanese way. If we're smart enough, we'll listen. We'll look at that success and realize what we must do is evolve. In business schools throughout the world in the 1970s and in particular in the 1980s, everybody was turning Japanese.

In fact, there was more to it than that. The 1970s really seemed to prove the point to just about everyone that the Western economic models, those economies that had been the miracle economies, the places where the Industrial Revolution was born, it really seemed like their time had passed. They started to stagnate in a very pronounced way. It wasn't just that they were stagnating while everybody else was stagnating; they were beginning to have really severe problems that they hadn't seen before. It was a real crisis of faith in the West and in particular in the United States. The economy of the 1970s in the United States was really lackluster, boring, and dull—it had lots of problems. You had 2 big problems to begin with. In 1973 and again in 1979, oil prices tripled. It was the success of the OPEC cartel that enabled them to triple, but it really put a stranglehold on all the economies in the world, but it was felt very sharply in the United States. As a result, we had very slow growth, an economy that ebbed and flowed up and down, but there was no real progress.

At the same time, we also had a period where we had relatively high inflation, so it wasn't just that we had high unemployment and a lackluster economy, we also had high inflation—2 bad things that almost never seem to go together. Usually you get one or the other; the 1970s gave us both. It got so bad that they even created a way to describe how bad things were. In the United States, we had something called the misery index, which is the unemployment rate plus the inflation rate. We were obsessed with the idea that we'd lost our way and things were bad and going to stay that way. When we think of the 1970s, particularly the late '70s, we think about malaise and a flat dull economy that had nowhere to go.

You might say that the world was really prime to believe in a new model of growth, to believe that there was a new way and that certainly the folks that had it before, the United States, Western Europe, they didn't have it at all. We were all ready for the change, and we were all ready to speak Japanese and get ready for the change. That's how certain we all were. I'll never forget that when I was in college, in the '80s, my college roommate for 4 years wanted to be in finance. At that period of time, 9 of the 10 largest banks in the world were Japanese banks. What did he do? He took Japanese like everybody else. They were kind of smug about it, all those guys taking Japanese. They said, gee, Peter, if you really want to work at finance or in economics, you might as well join the team, start speaking Japanese. We're all going to have to do it eventually.

Think back at how successful Japan had been. Recall that from 1950 to about 1990, per capita gross domestic product—that's the real income levels of individuals on average, it's the slices of pie I was talking about—grew at about 6% per year in inflation adjusted terms. That's really extraordinary. Like most of the world, they had their own slowdown in the 1970s, but it didn't last as long in others, and it didn't take as much wind out of their sails as it did most of their peer economies. Throughout the 1970s and into the 1980s, they really began to gain ground. All those famous brands—the Hondas, Toyotas, Sonys—really became household words around the world. We all began to think, gosh it's true; it has to be true. This excitement, this hyperbole, this belief in Japan's model continued all the way up through the very end of the 1980s. In fact in 1989 and in 1990, the hyperbole was really at a peak, and it was something you could feel absolutely everywhere.

Then, as they say, something happened. It seemed like a hiccup at first, but maybe it was more than that. It seemed like perhaps this great model was beginning to shake at the foundations, at least just a little bit. As it turned out, the shaking was caused by something that's actually pretty familiar. It's something that all economies face or at least all human normal mortal economies face. Japan had a really big property bubble. In all the excitement of that 40 years of spectacular growth, buying land in Japan became something of a good investment and then a pastime and then a fanatic pursuit to have land in the one economy in the world that was surging above all others. There was a cocktail that was mixed in Japan because part of their strategy for growth was to have really low interest rates. Why is that a strategy for growth? Low interest rates make it easier to borrow money, make it easier for your firms to grow and build and take over other parts of the world and compete against their peer nations. You had great excitement, an economy booming absolutely off the charts, low-interest rates as part of a strategy, and you had this huge surge in property values.

It was hard to overstate just how big that surge was. There were some real stories and even some apocryphal stories at the time that in Tokyo about 6 city blocks had the absolute value in terms of dollars that was even more than all the value of all the commercial property in the state of California. It was a pretty big property bubble. Even though people were super convinced that Japan would always be strong and always succeed, at least a few begin to think this is crazy. These prices are too high. Then, something bad began to happen, and it always happens with bubbles—they stop buying as much, the bubble began to shake and wobble, and eventually it burst.

The way property bubbles usually end is very bad, and it's part and parcel of the way they actually also rise. There's a little secret that happens in property bubbles, and it happens in Japan and in other countries and in the United States whenever there's this excess enthusiasm and very low interest rates. There's a financial term that you're familiar with, even if you don't think you're familiar with, called leverage. It's the real secret to bubbles growing high and being very difficult to live in when they shrink. Let me say that again—everybody's probably heard that word about leverage. I'd say that even if you don't think you know what it is, I bet you know how it works.

works like this. If you ever bought a home, you know something about leverage. Let's take a really simple example. Let's suppose you're going to buy a home, and it's a $100,000 home. Let's say that like most people, almost everybody around the world, you don't actually just pay cash for the whole thing, you put down 20% as a down payment, $20,000, and you borrow the other $80,000. That is exactly an example of leverage. It's really simple. You own something, this $100,000 home, that's worth actually 5 times as much as you've paid for it at the beginning. You're entitled to all the return from this asset that's worth 5 times what you paid for it at the beginning.

That's important because you have to go through this thought experiment. Suppose that home rises in value over one year from $100,000 to $110,000. How have you done on your investment? It sounds pretty simple. The home rose in value 10%, but if you think about it, you only put $20,000 down for that home. What you would get now if you sold the home and we sort of fudged the math about the loan that you still owe, you'd have a home at 110, pay off a loan for 80, and you get to keep 30. In fact, that's a 50-percent return on your investment. You put down 20 and now you have 30. Even though the home rose in value by 10%, your investment rose by 50, and that's the magic of leverage. You could imagine how good that is if you'd only put down 10% when in fact your investment would have risen by 100% in that same example.

In a market like Japan's when prices keep rising and rising and banks are willing to lend to you, and you can engage in a very simple form of leverage, just imagine what corporations can do and financially astute practitioners can do. They can have leverage of 100 to 1 and so when prices are going up, it's the ultimate casino, and everybody's intoxicated with the growth. I'll give you a little example about how much growth there was, and it's by looking at the stock market in Japan. At its peak in 1990, the Nikkei Index, which is the equivalent of the Dow Jones Industrial Index or the S&P 500, peaked at an index number at about 40,000, a really high number. In fact, the number had been only about 20,000 just 2 or so years earlier, so it had doubled in about 2 years. That's extraordinary for a broad basket of stocks. What's even more extraordinary than that is that about 20 years later in 2010 that index would be at about 9,500, just a little under ¼ of what it was at its peak 20 years earlier.

What we can say is that the miracle of Japan really came to a full, complete, and abrupt stop. Suddenly everything seemed to be going wrong. It wasn't just a hiccup. The Nikkei began to plummet and plummet quickly. Property values began to plummet and plummet quickly. In an economy that had 40 years of confidence built up, that had every reason to believe that it would never falter, that it would never sway, that had the expectation built in and supported by people around the world that said you will be the world leader, chart a new path, be the richest economy, everybody began to question that. That economy and that miracle absolutely seemed to be over. Most hoped that it wouldn't last for very long. Most hoped that it would be like a lot of recessions. As I've said before, and I would say again, a recession is a perfection normal thing. It just sometimes happens. This period of 6 months maybe up to 18–20 months when an economy seems to retreat, regroup, and slow down, but then restart is not so unusual. But, this recession was different. It didn't go away at all. It wasn't that short-term 18-month to 24-month. It was much longer than that. It was no hiccup. It was not heartburn. It was a heart attack, and it hit Japan very, very hard.

What was the problem? You would think that most economies when they're experiencing recession engage in some sort of plan to rebound it. In fact the Japanese did, but they had a classic economic problem to confront. Even with their good strategy and successful scheme for growing that economy, they really couldn't deal with it. The plot goes something like this. Whenever an economy is recovering from a huge asset decline, let's say a bubble bursting like property values going from a super high level to a much lower level in a short period of time, you have this real serious problem. It's a classic problem of falling asset values and then deflation, and it's really hard to overcome.

It works a little bit like this. Let's look back to that example of leverage. We took a very positive approach and said you buy this house, it's $100,000, it goes up by 10% over a year, and you feel great. You get that $10,000, which represents a 50% return on your investment if you put 20% down. It's that great leverage story. The problem with leverage is that it works wonderfully on the way up and just as awfully on the way down. Take that example again. Take a house that starts at $100,000 and in the course of a year goes down to $90,000. It's the same loss, it's a 10-percent fall, but you now have lost half of your investment. Remember, you put down 20, you owe 80, so a house that sells at 90 leaves you with only 10 to spare. That was happening all around Japan. As property values begin to fall and then begin to fall really quickly, all these leveraged individuals, all these leveraged companies, and all these leveraged financially astute wizards and masters of the universe begin to confront this classic problem. They couldn't pay off their debts. Property values fell so far and so fast that the thin margin of leverage people had protecting them, those small down payments, began to be eroded super quickly.

As a result, this adds fuel to the fire. This is fuel to the fire of deflation. Think of it this way. You have a home and the property values are high and you bought at the peak of the market, and then they start to plummet and fall. Do you think anybody wants to buy a home just when home prices begin to fall? Do you ever think about buying at that moment? Think in your mind what it means. When should you buy an asset value? When do you want to most buy it—at its peak or at its trough? Like anybody else, no matter the story, you want to buy when it's low. You want to buy when the only way forward is up. When those property values are falling, everybody wants to sell at the same time, and that makes the problem even more difficult to escape from. It makes the virus of a property bubble collapsing even more virulent. Property values fall, people panic so they sell even more, and they cut their prices even harder, and people wait even longer to buy because they're falling even faster. You never want to catch a falling knife, as they say. Nobody wants to buy on the way down. If you're falling from a really high peak, that could be a long way. As a central bank and a central government trying to deal with that, that's a very difficult issue to overcome.

What do you do to deal with that? One of the first casualties of any property bubble, and this was the casualty in Japan, were the banks. After all, the banks were the ones who supplied the money to pay for all those properties to begin with. They were the ones enabling the leverage to begin with. What did they find? Very soon and very shortly after the bubble began to collapse, they experienced a classic problem, a problem we saw in the United States during the Great Depression and would see again with what began as the Sub Prime Crisis in 2007. The banks that made these loans realized the values they had loaned to were just way, way off. It wasn't just that they were off on a little bit or a small fraction of the property, they were off on virtually all the loans they had made over the last 10 years.

They had no way to recoup their losses in short order and this led to another particular problem. Remember, these were 9 of the 10 largest banks in the world, so when they were collapsing everyone thought someone has to act, and the Japanese government was one of the first that needed to act. After all, they had worked together. Remember, one of the strengths of the Japanese model was cooperation between government and business—not a hands-off approach, a hands-on approach. A deal that said government will support you. We're not going to work in silos. We're going to work together.

All the banks thought—and rationally so—if we're failing, who do we look to? The Japanese government. They have to bail us out. They did their very best to do so because the deal, the strategy that Japan had crafted, really didn't include failures like these. The conglomerates in Japan, the so-called Keiretsu, these families of firms in related industries usually centered around a large bank, all wanted help. They were all suffering in a way they never expected, and they looked to the government to save them. If they couldn't expect the government to help them, then everyone would've lost faith. So, the government did the only thing that seemed rational—they stepped in, in a very big way. Their faith, all that buy-in, depended on the growth story that had manifested itself over 40 years and absolutely no one wanted to disappoint. Did they act? Absolutely, they acted in a very, very big way.

In a crisis like this, governments can learn from the examples of other countries. It certainly appeared that in Japan they had learned from the example of the Great Depression in the United States. They had a lot of economic history to look at. They looked back at that economy and its great collapse in the 1930s, and asked what would they have done if they knew what we know now? What the Japanese did was what we might call a very activist, very Keynesian, if you will, approach to saving the economy. They didn't take the classical approach, which would've been let it happen, let prices fall, and eventually the market will correct itself. They took the "in the long run, we're all dead" approach, and said we need to act in a big way.

There are 2 basic things that you can do, and they did both. One of them was what we call a massive monetary easing, which is kind of a formal way of saying they injected lots of money into the banking system and out into the economy. When the banks were flailing and failing and struggling, they began to pull back and not offer loans. Those loans are really the lifeblood of most business. In order to prevent the banks from pulling back and thereby strangling local business and the Keiretsu, the government decided to go in and make money all that much more available. They injected lots of money into the system to try to keep interest rates low—really, really low. In fact, they sent interest rates all the way down to virtually zero; one-tenth of 1% was the bottom and even that wasn't far enough to really get the economy started.

It's interesting because while we think of that as a very active government approach, that idea is what we might call a Monetarist idea. It's something that was really born out of a seminal work of a great economist of the 20th century, Milton Friedman, and his colleague Anna Schwartz. They wrote in their classic tome, *A Monetary History of the United States*, that the principle cause of the enduring Great Depression—the one thing that led it from a recession of a few years to a depression of 10 years—was the fact that the money supply collapsed, that the central bank didn't act by easing money and injecting money into the system. That's what the Japanese did in a huge way. Not so much later in the Sub Prime Crisis of 2007, the United States would follow suit. That was one thing they did. They really stepped on the accelerator in terms of the monetary side of the economy.

The other thing the Japanese did is they engaged in massive economic expenditures from the center of the government. They had a national debt that was actually relatively modest at the beginning of their problems, about 40% of GDP. A decade later, because of all the spending they needed to do—they tried to do to lift the economy to get prices going up and up again—they had a debt to GDP ratio of 140%. They had added an extraordinary amount of debt, they had added an incredible amount of money, and all in an effort to get this economy jumpstarted again.

In some ways, this was a continuation of their strategy of being very active and very involved. It evidenced their belief in this sort of Keynesian idea that what you need to do when the economy isn't working is get prices moving upward. Think about how you might do that, and think about what it means. Why would it be good to have prices moving upward? On the one hand, it helps people to decide that they now want to spend, and they don't want to stop spending. They don't want to hold back their money; they want to go ahead and use it. When you think prices are rising, it's advantageous to spend your money today before those prices rise. The problem in a recession is prices are headed in the other direction, and so the government tries to do something to stop that. One thing it can do is buy all things itself and make those prices rise through its own purchases, and that's what they did. The other thing it can do is inject lots of money into the system to try to put so much money into the hands of the population that prices have to rise by sheer inflation. That was really a big strategy of the Japanese government, to ensure people that the good times were going to return.

Did it work? No is the real short answer. Just like the United States, just like that loss decade of growth between 1929 and 1940 if not more, Japan embarked upon this great loss decade. It in fact lasted longer than that. They lost their miracle. They lost everything. The idea that Japan was the leading light, that it would one day not only reach the highest pinnacle of economic growth and income, but surpass it, teach everyone in the world a new better way, really evaporated in just a few years. Japan went from being the story to the side story to almost no story at all. Impossible as it is to believe, if you lived in the 1980s, and if you remember all the products and all the technology that came out of Japan, can you possibly imagine that the Internet boom, the technological boom, that cell phones and all of these things really didn't start in Japan, but somewhere else? That all of that growth and all of that wonderful economic activity that took place surrounding this new way to live and work was not in Japan, but somewhere else? I don't think anybody would've made that bet in 1989. I know I wouldn't have.

Another result that happened was Japan ended up being massively in debt. It was still a strong economy, and it was strong enough to endure that level of debt, but all the government spending really didn't make a difference. The Japanese growth story ended in 1989, and they went through a period where there was no more growth for about 10 years, despite the fact that they ended up with massive debt, and that overhang of debt is still their burden today.

What it implies for Japan is that they'll have to raise taxes, and they did. You have to have taxes to pay for that debt. What did you get for it? It was certainly not growth, and that's a real problem. Oddly enough, they didn't even get inflation, which is one thing they were actually trying to manufacture. As ironic as it sounds, in the midst of a recession, trying to manufacture some inflation can be a good thing. If I believe prices are not going to fall, but rise—that is, if I believe that there will be inflation—I'm encouraged to spend again. Japan got the opposite. They got deflation. In fact, they couldn't push interest rates any lower. They'd lowered them to already zero and below that you really can't do anything. In some sense, all they managed to do was eventually stop the bleeding. The growth never returned.

Looking at this great success story, maybe the great success story of the 20th century, and then looking at this great fall from grace, what are the lessons that we can take away? There seem to be a few lessons we can take away from Japan. One of the simple lessons, or at least one that we can now look back and say that seems certainly wrong, was that they shouldn't have bled out the losses of their banks. They waited a very long time to realize, to let those banks absorb all the bad loans that they'd made and fail or just simply fade away. They tried to hold on and hold on in the belief that if they held on a little bit longer the market would come back, the values would come back, and ultimately they wouldn't have to take that pain of writing off the value of very, very over-inflated assets. That seemed to be a very difficult thing for them to do. They waited far too long and it seems to have stifled their economy for many, many years. Maybe it was the principal cause of the enduring nature of that great recession in Japan.

A second thing is that the dynamism, that animal spirit that really seemed to motivate Japan over 40 years, is a real necessary component. Once you lose it, it's really hard to get back. It's magic, in some sense, but it's also based on strong investments and fundamentals and high savings rates and good labor and the like. But, Japan lost that magic over a few years. After that point, there's really not much you can do. They tried to hold onto that story even longer, but that dynamism never really returned.

The last thing maybe we can say is that bubbles are absolutely deadly. Letting property values or asset values of any kind rise that high beyond what seems reasonable seems to be able to topple any economy, even the world leaders at just about any time. In that sense, Japan seemed just as vulnerable to all the ills that had befallen other economies—free-market economies, not the mixed economies with governments and business working together. Those things seemed to fall on Japan just as they did to others.

The last lesson might be that deflation is absolutely paralyzing. When people believe that prices are going to fall and keep falling, then they hold back. In holding back, they propel prices downward even further. This negative spiral can last a long time. We have 2 great examples from 2 of the world's leading economies. It reminds one of the great words of President Franklin Roosevelt who said, "The only thing we have to fear is fear itself." In that he was talking about pulling back so far that we actually made our problems worse, not better.

Where is Japan at the end of the day? Despite that huge fall from grace, despite all the things that happened over the period of the 1990s, they're still really a rich country. They're still among the richest. They manage to have so much growth that they held even and flat, but they're still more or less where they were. They didn't take big steps back; they just took no steps forward. What that proved in some sense is that their model really wasn't superior, that there wasn't a new way to do things that would burst through the lead of the world economies and set a new standard for world income levels and per capita growth. Japan's model seemed to be as vulnerable to ills as any other, and it couldn't take that lead. It seemed to be evidence that perhaps a free-market approach, or one approach that involved less government entanglement with business, was equally successful. It's interesting how fast we went from a crisis of faith in the United States wanting to change everything to be Japanese to a belief that we had it right all along, and this was destined to happen.

The strategy that the Japanese pursued, like in many other economic strategies whether they be free market or government involved, just wasn't consistent with macroeconomic fundamentals like asset prices. They paid the ultimate price for that. The religion that we had around the strategy of Japan was a big mistake. We looked at that and saw this great growth and presumed that everything would follow from it, that it really had no weaknesses, that it was wearing bulletproof iron and that nothing could penetrate that economic model, but the truth was different. We learned that with the Japanese example. We also learned that investors, when they make mistakes about property values on a large scale over time, the results can be very, very costly. Those things are to be avoided at all cost, especially when people are buying into a story, and the story seems to propel itself. The story of Japan in fact proved to be better than the reality. The proof was really hard to take, particularly for the Japanese.

What lessons does that give us today? In closing we could say that no one really knows what the economic models of Japan will look like in the future or whether or not they'll teach us that in fact they are less vulnerable to some of the other ills that befall other strategies and other economies. Perhaps it's a lesson that all glory passes and that no economy, no leader, is ever invulnerable. In fact, that seems to be the case with Japan. Perhaps the biggest lesson is eventually you can't hide your losses. Whatever economic model a country has, whatever strategy it pursues, it's never perfect. A good economy just like a good organism, just like a good company, must always adapt and adapt quickly to changing circumstances or else pay the very highest costs.

# From Closed to Open Economies
## Lecture 10

**Something very profound began to happen at the very end of the 20th century that really changed all of our ideas about what the world would look like going forward. So important were the changes that began to take place, so important were the countries in which those changes began to take place, that most of us believe it will change the world economic order for centuries.**

Until the time of the Industrial Revolution, economic power generally equaled the size of the country. Then, starting in about the mid-18th century, relatively small countries, such as England, France, and Germany, grew very large in terms of total economic output. At the same time, the giants of the world, such as China and India, weakened considerably. These historically strong economies, with rich cultures and abundant resources, fell farther and farther behind, and it seemed that they would never catch up. Relative to most of the world, where material living standards were rising, the economies of China and India were almost completely impoverished.

Part of the explanation for the decline of these economies may have been their aversion to free markets. China, for example, was a complete **command economy**, one in which the central government made all relevant economic decisions. For this reason, China absorbed almost none of the advances of the Industrial Revolution and experienced virtually no growth for nearly 100 years. Then, in the mid-1970s, during the boom of the Asian Tigers, the Chinese leader Deng Xiaoping decided it was time for China to change course. He instituted incentives for farmers and encouraged experimentation around the margins of the command economy. The result was amazing growth.

In the late 1970s, China began to open its markets to external trade, entering the world economy with a huge population that would work for very low wages. All the production that flowed to the Asian Tigers as the workshops of the world began to flow into China. This, in turn, energized the population further and solidified the experimentations and reforms. China also invested in infrastructure, which led to further productivity. In a sense, the country was leading itself into its own Industrial Revolution.

The story in India was slightly different. Although India became a democracy after it gained its independence, it took for its economic model the Soviet Union. The Indian government exercised strict central control of the economy up until the fall of the Soviet Union, when it became apparent that this approach was fatally flawed. In 1990, India teetered on the brink of collapse. But again, a leader, Finance Minister Manmohan Singh, saw the need for change and began to implement straightforward plans to open the economy and allow India to trade more freely in the world.

Both India and China had a degree of political stability, which ensured that people bought into the changes taking place. India also opened itself at an early stage of the information technology revolution, to which it was able to apply its abundance of human talent. When Indians who had emigrated to other countries saw the emergence of growth, they began to send money back home to fund additional investment. These two economies now have the potential to revolutionize the world. Through increased openness, they can earn foreign exchange currency, which they can invest around the world and solidify their own economies. In short, they can become richer and take bigger stakes in the small economies that surpassed them centuries before. ∎

**If we look at what happened, we can say that these two economies [China and India], in their opening up, have great potential. If their potential is what the potential was of the Asian Tigers, if they can match growth rates of Japan decades earlier, they'll revolutionize the entire world.**

## Important Term

**command economy**: An economy in which the central government makes all relevant economic decisions.

Prahalad, *The Fortune at the Bottom of the Pyramid.*
Rajan and Zingales, *Saving Capitalism from the Capitalists.*
Yergin and Stanislaw, *The Commanding Heights.*

### Questions to Consider

1.  How will the world likely change with its two most populous nations growing faster than ever before in their history?

2.  What kept China and India from rapid growth for the first 200 years of the period of modern economic growth?

# From Closed to Open Economies
## Lecture 10—Transcript

Welcome back. Until about the last decade of the 20th century, the broad world story of economic modernity that moved from the Dark Ages to modern economic growth could almost be completely summarized by the very basic story of the Industrial Revolution. We could look at the economies of England and Western Europe. We could look at their colonies and their largest offshoots like the United States, Australia, New Zealand, and understand most of the course of modern economic history. But, that's just not true anymore. Something very profound began to happen at the very end of the 20th century that really changed all of our ideas about what the world would look like going forward. So important were the changes that began to take place, so important were the countries in which those changes began to take place, that most of us believe it will change the world economic order for centuries.

The growth in the last decade of the 20th century was absolutely amazing. In fact, if you looked at any period of total economic growth—by that I mean let's think about all the countries of the world and summing their growth together—that was the fastest period of global economic growth in all of recorded history. It changed all of our ideas about how growth emerges and about what overall growth means and where it resides. Until that last decade, we had this idea more or less settled in our minds. There were some economies that were much better suited to growth, and those were mostly the economies of the Industrial Revolution. There were a few others like the Asian Tigers that seemed to grab onto ideas, but they were actually relatively small economies—not tiny, but relatively small. That meant that their growth didn't really upset the balance of the world. That would've been true, and that was the story that most of us were prepared to carry into the 21st century, but late in the game in the 1980s and the 1990s, all that began to change in a very big way. Part of that profound way involves 2 of the largest economies in all of world history, China and India.

For most of world history economic power really equaled the size of the country, and there's a pretty simple reason for that. If you think about a world in which incomes aren't that different across countries, where everybody's income level is about the same irrespective of what region they live in or what country they live in, then a large population means a lot of economic output and a lot of economic power. In fact, that was the way that the world looked mostly up until the Industrial Revolution, which really upset that balance. In fact, what we had in that period was very large economies in terms of total amount of economic output in relatively small countries—countries like England, France, and Germany. They weren't small relative to lots of their peers, but they were very small relative to the giants of the world, the Chinas and the Indias. Those economies were at least 10 times as large and, rather than being economically powerful during this period, they actually became economically much more weak.

It's an interesting point, but when most of us talk about the Industrial Revolution, we think about it from the vantage point of the winners, of the countries that grew and became powerful and strong. But, in fact the Revolution wasn't really just these countries getting powerful and strong; it was the fact that some of the giants in all of world history became relatively powerless and weak. So much so was this change that it really upset the world balance where economic size really meant economic output and not overall population. It wasn't the size of the pie all together that we begin to measure, but the size of the slices, the wealth of the individuals. In that sense, the Industrial Revolution meant that the West surged ahead, and much of the East was left very far behind.

It meant that the seats of world power, that the giants of the world economy, really gave way to countries like Europe and the United States—relatively young countries and relatively small. If you look at a world map, and you look at the countries in and around Europe, they look almost like little peninsulas off a broader Asian continent. That's really what they were—not so big in population and certainly throughout most of history not all that technologically advanced relative to countries in the Middle East and in the East. But, the Industrial Revolution really upset that balance. It meant that these countries that were smaller and seemed more backward for a long period of time took the lead. In fact it appeared that they would take the lead and not give it back.

What's perhaps more astounding is that all the while they were taking the lead and growing rapidly economically, the giants of the world, the Chinas and the Indias, really never caught up. They fell behind and fell further behind and further behind, and it seemed as if they were never going to get started to catch up. It really begged a large question: Why were the largest economies of the world, or at least historically in the world, and ones that had so much technological advance, such rich cultures, such bright minds and abundant resources, why were they falling so far behind these tiny economies? These giants really became Lilliputians almost overnight. China and India represented more than 80% of total world output for most of recorded history. But, beginning with the Industrial Revolution in the late-18th century and early-19th century, they begin to slide really sharply. These giants went from being 80% of the world economy down to 60 and 50 and 40 and further and further to where they almost became insignificant. Amazingly, economies with hundreds of millions of people, with vast resources and amazing trade and commercial capabilities, actually begin to become less and less important in the world. They really lost all their seat of world power in a relatively short period of time.

This is the other side of the Industrial Revolution. It's the loss of power and influence. Maybe that's one of the most important outcomes. That's the true revolution that economies that were powerful, countries that were powerful, became a lot less powerful, and these smaller countries really in some sense took over much of the world. That's a real revolution. While we see the Industrial Revolution as a great success, and indeed it was in terms of the ability to raise human living standards, it also represented a tremendous reversal. It was a reversal that endured, endured throughout not only the 19th century, but into the 20th century, the greatest period of economic growth and almost all the way throughout it. So much so that most of us thought it might not ever turn around.

Things actually got so bad in China and India, living standards actually failed to grow so much, that by some measures they even got worse during that period. As amazing as it seems, it appears that in these 2 economies that held so many secrets of the world that their living standards actually got worse while most of the rest of the world got at least a little better and some of the world lived much, much better.

When living standards fell so far so fast, it also meant that commercial output in these economies became smaller, and that their commercial weight in the world became weaker. I wouldn't say that they became insignificant, but they became almost insignificant throughout the world. At least in terms of commercial output, these economies really drew no water. They couldn't compete with even small economies like England. Even Belgium seemed to have a greater economic weight in the world than in some ways did China and India. They became economically insignificant at the same time and through the same fashion that their populations really entered into vast states of poverty. Relative to most of the world, where living standards were rising, at least material living standards, the economies of China and India were almost completely impoverished. By the middle part of the 20th century because of the large populations in these 2 countries, we could say that approximately 40% of the whole world population lived in poverty. Most of those who were impoverished lived in China, India, and Africa.

Somehow these countries really missed out. There was a century of amazing growth, a century of growth from 1870–1970 at least, and none of it occurred in these 2 nations. Not only did they fail to grow a little, they failed to really grow at all. Their problems, if anything, seemed to grow much, much worse. It was so much worse that for many of us, when we looked at poverty in China and India, we said it's endemic. It will always be true. That flies in the face of history, but it actually seemed that it had always been true.

In fact, I can remember that when I was younger and in fact when many of you were younger, you might recall that we associated poverty and struggle with these economies more than any other. I can think about mothers sitting around the table at dinnertime looking at their kids and looking at plates where a lot of good food wasn't consumed. The child is about to walk away, and before he walks away, what does the mother say? Finish your food. Clean your plate. Don't you know there are starving children in—and for most families they would probably say China. For a lot of recorded history and deep into the 20th century, that was true. In fact, in one of the most tragic events in history if not economic history, China embarked upon plans like the Great Leap Forward where agriculture was collectivized. The plan was so disastrous economically and in terms of productivity and output that at least 10 million people starved to death. It's a really profound collapse of an economy that was once strong. In the midst of a world that was more productive than ever, it continued to struggle, and India did as well. Poverty was endemic and seen everywhere. Every image one had of poverty probably had mostly an Asian face associated with it at least throughout the 1970s.

This raises a big question for us: Why were these 2 giant economies now Lilliputians? What is it that they really did so wrong? How could not any of the good of the Industrial Revolution seem to rub off on them? Even if they didn't follow the same economic strategies, even if they didn't have the same political beliefs or national leaders, weren't there technological advances that would've advanced their lives? Weren't there some obvious wins that could be implemented anywhere and make them look better? One would think so, but it seemed just not to be true. Something was wrong and continued to go wrong for long enough that for the most part everyone was desperate, particularly in those economies, to look for change. It's really hard to say what really happened to set these economies on the bad course to no growth, but it seems to start with their history and a real aversion to free markets—not a full aversion in all cases, but a real aversion to engaging in basic economic activity.

When I say that these economies seemed to have an aversion to markets, that's a bit of an understatement. China certainly had much more than just an aversion to markets. They were really completely shut off to markets. This was a great example of a real command economy. When I say a command economy, I mean an economy in which a central government really makes, for all practical purposes, all the real relevant economic decisions. In China, they had not just a little lack of openness, but a thorough lack of openness. It was almost completely closed. There was no real trade between China and proximate nations or distant nations. There was no real trade even within China in some cases because that's not what the government wanted. The command economy stated otherwise.

For that reason, because it was closed or perhaps protected, many of us thought that it was just shut off from all the benefits, and that seemed to be true. Being completely shut off to markets, China didn't absorb many of the advances in the rest of the world either because it considered them not necessary or because it simply wasn't aware of them, or the ideas weren't democratized to enough people. But China absorbed almost none of the great advances of most of the Industrial Revolution and relatively few of the technological advances as well. That lack of openness, that more than a little aversion to markets, cost China very dearly. They paid a really heavy price. For being heavily closed, growth virtually stopped for nearly 100 years.

What happened? To go from completely closed to the zenith that China became, what really occurred? What really forced them to make the change? That's a very long story, and it's something that we'll return to in subsequent lectures. It deserves a lot of time and attention, but I'll see if I can get there a little bit quickly so that we can learn a little bit from the Chinese and the Indian example. What really seemed to happen was that, in the mid 1970s, at a point when China was deeply impoverished, when it was obvious to everyone, including leaders like Deng Xiaoping, that there was nothing going right, that poverty was in China and was staying in China and none of the 5-year plans were succeeding and eradicated. Deng really just basically decided it's time to do something different. It's time for China to change course in a big way, and that's exactly what he did.

You can think about this in terms of other stories we've told; think about this in the context of regional economic history. If you're Deng Xiaoping and if you have the ability to really look out around the region and see economic activity and success, what would you see? You'd see a lot of Asian Tigers, for one. You'd see an economy like Taiwan, and you'd see it growing rapidly and people getting richer year in and year out. You'd see that economy growing a lot more powerful and more relevant to the world. You'd see its name stamped on the bottom of all manner of manufactured goods and wonder how could they do that? How can they live so well when we don't? Aren't those effectively our same people, nearly our same culture, if not exactly our same culture? What's really different seems to be not important because we could copy the Taiwanese model, couldn't we?

Or, even look at Singapore, growing even more rapidly and even smaller and less significant to the world. How could such a tiny city nation be so relevant and grow so rich when China, in all its richness and all its size and power, remains so poor? When Deng looked around at the world, he would see Chinese diaspora flourishing everywhere, and he would see Chinese suffering inside his own borders. What he began to do was look at those examples and try to emulate at least a little bit of what they'd done. It's a very natural thing, but it took a lot of courage, and it took a lot of courage for Deng to stay the course even amid a lot of criticism. But, in the midst of poverty, he was desperate and so were so many Chinese people.

One of the simplest things that Deng did was he recognized that people needed incentives. He had ways of putting this. He said people need incentives to grow because when they're fighting for themselves and their loved ones and their own family, when they are working for things that they can keep at home, then they'll invest more heavily. It's a very natural idea. He did something really relatively simple. He started with a largely peasant rural economy and said you produce for the state, you produce in a commanded economy, and you produce a quota of agricultural output. But, rather than focus only on that quota, let me do the following. Let me allow you to keep any excess production you have on the farm. You'll be given a quota, and you'll still owe your due to the state and to the community at large, but anything extra is yours. That extra you can use to sell or to trade or whatever you want.

This incentive to begin to have something for oneself beyond what the state demanded seemed to be enough to fully energize so much of the talented and energetic Chinese population. They began to think more critically about how to reorganize their farms, about how to reorganize the way they produced and what they produced and where they would sell, so that they could win, so that they could engage in a very basic simple entrepreneurial activity. Deng Xiaoping encouraged lots of experimentation around the margins of a relatively cohesive Chinese command economy. Rather than fully revolutionize it—this wasn't a shock therapy approach where he introduced free markets overnight—he tinkered at the margins. At the margins he saw amazing success and amazing growth.

They were opening for the first time. A little bit of success at the margin in a few countries and in a few regions led to lots of success. Suddenly Chinese production of agricultural products was skyrocketing in a very real way. It was obvious why; people responded to these incentives. They liked the idea. They had better plans and had been restricted from implementing them.

They started to open their markets not just to trade internally, but externally as well. This was important because it was a rich economy in one sense. It had a great amount of human capital—very simple and basic skills, but tangible skills and skills that were available to the world at very, very low wages. China entered the world economy for the first time in a meaningful way in the late 1970s. It did so with an energized population that would work at very low wages, so competitive that all the production that had flowed to the workshop of the world throughout the Asian Tigers now began to slowly flow into China. That energized further and solidified the beginnings of these experimentations and these reforms around the margin.

They also engaged in a huge investment in infrastructure. There's that magic again. With a great infrastructure, in an economy that had virtually no solid roads, weak port systems, and very little airport systems, Chinese government officials began to solidify and collect resources so that they could develop a world-class infrastructure. Why is that beneficial? Why is an infrastructure so important? Infrastructure helps lead to productivity. The more efficient are our roads and all the transportation systems, the better and the easier we can operate and work and live. China, by opening slowly, generating incomes it had not had before, really began on this fairly normal wave of economic growth, taking new production, channeling it into productivity through infrastructure, and leading itself into the beginnings of its own Industrial Revolution. It was maybe 100 years late, but it started and, when it did, it had lots of momentum.

With India, you have a slightly different story. The Indian economy had lots of characteristics that many associated with great successful economies. It was a remarkable democracy. It's true that it had been independent only a relatively short time, but it did have a lot of the institutional characteristics that many seem to associate with the West. For that reason, many expected that the Indian economy would already be growing quickly, but in fact it wasn't. In fact, they also had a very closed economy. Rather than have a free-market approach after independence, the Indian economy really embarked upon a period of a very closed approach. Its economic idol, if you will, its model for growth was really much more rooted in the Russian model, in the model of the Soviet Union. The communist model said control things from the center, decide what's to be produced and where, and manage the economy with all the efficiency and all the technological talent that Indians had. All the mathematical skills or great statisticians could be brought to bear on formulating a grand plan. India followed that plan. They followed that plan all the way up until the collapse of the Soviet Union itself, when it became apparent to them and to everyone else that those plans just simply didn't work. They were fatally flawed.

It really took that huge collapse, that near complete collapse in 1990 and 1991, where India teetered on the brink, where it almost completely ran out of monetary reserves and had to endure the pain of a rapid devaluation. It took staring poverty in the face and recognizing that this model was fundamentally flawed for a new leadership to take hold. Finance Minister Manmohan Singh, who would become prime minister, began to implement very straightforward economic plans to open the economy, to reduce the bureaucracy and reduce the red tape, and allow Indians to trade more freely on the world. Here you have this sort of second revolution that looks similar. These 2 giants that had become Lilliputians begin to grow again when they did some of the very simplest things you can imagine; they just stopped closing themselves off. They just opened up a little bit, and the rest took care of itself it seemed.

As we know from previous examples, it's not enough just to open up and let things happen. It requires a lot of things to go right. One of the things that both economies seemed to have going right for them was stability. Both had enough economic and political stability throughout this period, although it could be tumultuous in some cases, to make sure that people could buy into the plan, that the opening was believed to be credible, and that it would endure. The investment it takes to really open up business and engage in competition, for the first time on a global scale in a real way, they could buy into that because you had that stability. In India they had lots of stability, even though it was a democracy that is in some ways very messy.

They also had a great opportunity because the timing was just about right. When India opened in earnest in the early 1990s, it was the beginning of a new surge in the information technology fields. There was a revolution that required so many of the talents that India had in abundance, if not overabundance. The confluence of those events, the coming together of that episode in human history and technological history, and the opening of India really helped solidify these reforms, lock in the stability, and begin to carry India out of the doldrums of poverty into a period of modern economic growth.

We'd known for years if not for decades, perhaps even longer, that the citizens of these 2 economies, Chinese and Indians, had fled for economic opportunity elsewhere. What they saw in their homelands were countries becoming weaker and slightly less powerful economically. When they had the chance, they migrated to other places. Just as the Chinese had succeeded in Singapore and in Taiwan and other places, the Indian diaspora had fled all around the world, particularly in Western Europe and also in the United States. When they saw growth begin to emerge in India for real for the first time, then they sent back lots of their funds to help fund that investment. They sent back all the monies that they had begun to earn in other countries that had been successful and helped solidify reforms, and set the course toward modern economic levels of development. That growing stability that came from these funds from the diaspora of these 2 economies fermented more and more investment and helped lock in reforms that India needed to endure.

What are the lessons we can take away from these 2 big examples, these giants that became Lilliputians that only very late in the 20th century decided that they could open up and maybe set the course to becoming giants again? If we look at what happened, we can say that these 2 economies, in their opening up, have great potential. If their potential is what the potential was of the Asian Tigers, if they can match growth rates of Japan decades earlier, they'll revolutionize the entire world. Their openness makes a huge difference. It makes a very big difference in the world. Why is that? Through their openness and the low wages that they have in their population, they can earn foreign exchange currency. That is, they can earn dollars and euros and pounds. With these currencies, they can begin to invest around the world and really solidify and modernize the economy. In short, they can become richer and take bigger stakes in the small economies that surpassed them centuries before.

When you think about it, the math is just amazing. Think about that. Japan really rocked through the world and changed the way we think about economic growth by growing at 6% per year in terms of per capita GDP for 40 years. China seems to be growing at the same rate, if not faster, but it's 10 times the size of Japan. If Japan had a big effect, what will China do? Think of India. It's growing as well—not quite as fast as China's been growing—but it's also 10, 11 times as large as Japan, which many would consider a reasonably large country in and of itself. The revolution that's taking place at the end of the 20$^{th}$ century is one that certainly seems it would change the course of the 21$^{st}$ century, at least in terms of economic output in the shape of the world economy.

What we can say at the end of the day is that trying the market approach in a really simple way—no magic formulas, just opening up, letting loose, getting grid of restrictions on private enterprise—seem to be enough to begin the economic reforms that will transport the United States and Western European nations from their current position perhaps back to the position they occupied before the revolution began. Maybe not, but that's one of the consequences that could occur, and it's one of the reasons why studying these 2 giant economies is so important. It also tells us that in these economies early wins were really necessary and really easy. All they had to do was to stop standing in the way of business. In the same way that we've described backward or low-income economies being able to race to the front and grow at high rates, we can think about these 2 giants that were very backward, that were very low income. All they had to do is stop getting in the way, open up a little bit, and they should have some growth.

Can it endure? So far it has, and there's good reason why. One of the other elements we've continued to talk about in terms of the secret recipe of economic growth is that political, that social buy-in. The buy-in by the populations in these 2 economies has been huge. With memories of profound poverty motivating support for these changes, this has to be so much better. People can think about making changes and complaining about this or that policy, but it's much better than where they were before. For that reason we think these reforms are here to stay. The course that these 2 giants have set upon in the last part of the 20$^{th}$ century seem likely to endure.

Where do we go next? The road ahead is certainly better for both economies. If they maintain the policies they've had thus far, their populations will grow richer, they'll grow more important, and they'll have much more of an economic base, much more of a cushion that can protect them when economic times grow hard. But, by the same token we know that throughout most of economic history, when we see economies race to the top, when they grow rapidly and when they converge upon the world leaders in terms of per capita income, the road gets a little bit harder. The reforms have to be a little bit deeper and more enduring. No longer are they as far behind as they were. They'll need to make deeper changes, more fundamental ones, and that's often the road to a rocky adolescence in terms of economic growth. If they'll be able to make the change, then they should be able to set upon the course that will lead them back to the leading economies of the world economy.

In closing, we can think about these 2 giants and the course of economic history that they've run. They went from being leaders in the world, they went from being leaders for centuries, while the world stayed at a relatively fixed state of economic development, but then they failed to adapt. As the revolution transformed lots of economies, smaller economies, less significant, less resource rich economies, they failed to adapt. It was only at least 100 if not 200 years after the beginning of that revolution that they begin to adapt in a way that really put them on the course and the right path. It teaches us that adaptation is never over, that no model is ever complete, and that no matter how big and how rich you are, you can lose your place if you're not careful.

# How Can We Manage Global Growth?
## Lecture 11

Think about it this way—some things that are really personal, the mortgage rate that you pay on your home, the rate that you buy your car with, the job that you hold, ... all heavily depend on actions that take place completely outside the United States, by people who don't live under your same laws and your same culture. That's a bit interesting, maybe disquieting, but it also offers lots of opportunities.

Without question, the world economy is much more connected than ever before. Our fates—the ways in which we live—depend not only on our fellow citizens but on people who live under different political and economic systems. Global financial markets are now almost perfectly integrated, no longer separated by ideologies or national borders. What happens in one financial market is exactly what happens almost automatically and instantaneously in another.

Having integrated, highly connected markets—one giant pool of savings and investment—means that people can earn more money from their wealth and can borrow at lower cost. It also means that those who live in an unstable economy don't have to suffer the consequences of having all their money tied up there. They can achieve a more balanced portfolio with stable investments in the economies of the West. These types of activities have always been beneficial to savers and investors, but they are not without costs. In such a "flat" world, we're a bit more exposed, and our competition is now virtually everyone.

Understanding the **balance of payments** helps us understand just how integrated the world is. The balance of payments measures the flow of resources—goods and services, as well as financial funds—from one economy into another and aggregates them around the world. It's the summary of any individual nation's economic relationship with the rest of the world. Components of the balance of payments include the **current account**, which provides information about the flow of goods and services, and the capital and financial account, which tells us about flows of financial resources.

We can see the degree to which we are living in a single world economy by examining some of the activities among the world's largest economies. The United States, for example, is a consumer-heavy country and has a large trade deficit. Others in the world use the excess cash we're sending them to buy our assets—stocks and bonds, companies, and land. For us, the result is lower interest rates

**All the markets around the world are just one big financial market. Buying and selling assets across borders—that's the definition of financial markets—it's one big pool and they operate absolutely seamlessly.**

and higher asset values. In this way, our fates—the value of our 401(k) accounts, for example—are determined by the actions of people in other countries. It's likely that this imbalance can't last forever, which means we'll have to export more, others will buy fewer of our assets, and our asset values will fall. These factors matter a lot for the shape, color, and character of our economy.

Integration also carries some risks. For example, a financial hiccup in one part of the world will be immediately felt in another. Integration also means that producers have the opportunity to sell in much bigger markets and have access to cheaper financing, but the costs here are connections to competitors around the world. Today, we live in a world that's much more like one giant economy than ever before. This more integrated, more connected, flatter world, offers us a world of benefits, but it asks an awful lot of us, too. We must learn much more about this integrated world to live peacefully in it and to prosper as we've done in previous decades. ∎

## Important Terms

**balance of payments**: An accounting system that measures the flows of resources from one economy into another and aggregates them across the world. Provides a summary of an individual nation's economic relationship with the rest of the world.

**current account**: One component of the balance of payments; provides information about the flow of goods and services in an economy.

## Suggested Reading

Bastiat, *Economic Fallacies*.

Faulkner and Shell, eds., *America at Risk*.

Friedman, *The World Is Flat*.

Grossman and Helpman, *Innovation and Growth in the Global Economy*.

Naim, *Illicit*.

Prahalad, *The Fortune at the Bottom of the Pyramid*.

## Questions to Consider

1. Is the world economy truly flat? What will be required of the United States and other Western nations to benefit from a more integrated global economy?

2. How does financial market integration affect daily life?

# How Can We Manage Global Growth?
## Lecture 11—Transcript

Welcome back. We've had a long discussion already about the many individual challenges that nations face when they try to grow. These growth challenges at the individual national level are really profound. They're very difficult, as is managing the complexity of political stability even within a small country that isn't beset by war or other extreme challenges. But, even if these countries get that right and manage their own internal policy successfully, even that won't be enough to ensure stability and growth over a long period of time. This is especially true in our modern, very global, very integrated, and connected economy. As it turns out, in the modern economy, it's not just what you do, it's not just the policies and laws that you pass and enact, it's what other countries do as well.

This lecture really explores the powerful and challenging connectedness of the global economy—the flatness of the global economy, if you will. We ask what it really means for individual nations and their efforts to grow. In particular, we're concerned with what it may mean for both high-income nations that are highly integrated with other nations of the world or perhaps the entire global economy, but we also want to know what it means for those developing economies, maybe especially those low-income economies that are struggling just to get it right internally. How does having a world that is so integrated and connected really influence their ability to raise living standards, eradicate poverty, and ensure stability? Is it easier than it was before, or is it harder? We've worked so hard to get the world to be integrated and open, but is it really a good thing?

There's really no question that the world economy is much more connected than ever before. Just think about the way that you live, think about the way that we operate, think about your phone, your computer, where you work, and where the other people you work with live and reside and do their jobs. Think about where you buy your products and where those products and services come from and who made them. It's obviously much more connected. Obviously our lives are much more integrated with the lives of individuals who live around the world in places that we've barely even heard of, much less understand or have some similarity to. But, what does all of that really mean? Is it an important fact? Is it something that affects the way that we live? Do we have to change policies and ideas, maybe even economic theories and schools of thought, to adjust to the idea that the world is just that much more connected than ever? When we say that the world is really flat, really connected, is that an important conclusion?

We can start down this road by trying to ask a bit more of a scientific question: How would we measure how connected that we are? How connected are we really? But, maybe even more so than that, what does it really mean? What is the value or the cost or the risk of being that connected? Until we get behind it a little bit and put some flesh on this skeleton of yes—we're much more connected; it's obvious technology makes it so—then we don't really have an awful lot to say. We don't really have something really tangible to say about how being connected, about how being integrated and more integrated than before, really makes our lives different, better, or maybe even more difficult.

We could begin by asking ourselves how much does our connectedness really matter and how do we think about being connected to the rest of the world? Do we think about it in human terms, about individual to individual? Is it something a bit more abstract, something that connects nations at their level and maybe collects policymakers and maybe armies or large corporations and multinationals, but what does that connectedness really mean? Does it come down to something as simple as where I choose to eat, how much I get paid, who I buy my car from, and the way that I live? In fact, it comes down to just about everything.

When we think about connectedness and how it's different in a modern 21st-century economy relative to economies of the past, we can begin by thinking about the way that we normally connect to other individuals, whether they're outside of our communities or outside of our region, states, or countries. The way that we connect to individuals in economics in any economy is through the marketplace. There are lots of different types of markets, and these markets are fundamentally the basic places, the venues where our decisions are connected to each other. When I say connected, what we really mean is that these are the places where we engage in some social fashion that actually connects our fates to one another. It means that we matter to each other, and that what's good for one of us can be good for the other or bad or challenging or just something we have to take into account.

Let's think at the beginning about something like goods markets, places where we buy and sell goods and services. Goods markets have existed since antiquity. We've always had marketplaces at the centers of town. We have malls today. We now even connect virtually online to just about any location around the planet. In the same way, in the selling and buying of goods and services around the world, we're actually deeply connected to all the nations of the world actually much, much more so than ever before. Our fates and where we buy things from and where we produce and sell things too are much different than ever before because the world is just that much more integrated.

The world is just an awful lot more integrated than it ever was before. We understand that because we buy and sell things to each other. But, the more plain and more reasonable way to think about this is to say that our fates—the way that I am able to live, the way that a citizen of India or China or Mexico or anywhere around the world is able to live—depend not just on people that are like them, not just on people that are near them, or that they are their citizens, or that have the same laws, customs, and norms applied to them, but also on people they may never meet, understand, or know, on people who live under vastly different political and economic systems. Their fates are exchanged in a way that they never could be before because there were barriers between the people that existed before. There were walls or complete ideologies that separated parts of the world.

After the late 20th century, most of these barriers came down and it meant that we were integrated, and our fates were connected in a much more diverse way to people we never contemplated being connected to. These were people that were just the subject of distant ideas, folklore, and stories. Today, they're our customers.

Goods markets are among the most integrated in the world. That means that the prices that we pay for goods and services depend much more so on what happens around the world than ever before. In other words, it doesn't just matter if I'm a citizen of California what wages they're getting for citizens of New York or Florida or Texas; it matters what they're getting in Mumbai and Delhi and in Shanghai and Kuala Lumpur and Rio de Janeiro and in Monterey, Mexico.

It matters because our goods markets are connected. By the same token, our labor markets are connected. That's the flow of people in jobs from one place to another. Goods are really connected, labor markets a little bit less so, and there's a good reason for that. Labor markets are less connected because people don't just want to pick up and move all the time. It's one thing to begin to sell to customers in Shanghai; it's another thing to move there to begin your work.

You have to change not just your language and your culture, but the very laws under which you're willing to live. Your entire culture might need to change. That means that labor markets are among the least integrated; yet they are integrated in ways we never examined and considered before. They're integrated, but they're slow to integrate. People can walk across borders, as they often do in the United States from Mexico and other points south. They can walk across borders like from East Germany to West, but they don't do this very rapidly, and today what's amazing is they don't even have to. They cannot have to walk across border and still connect to another economy by connecting virtually over the Internet through the satellite waves. I can work just about anywhere and deliver my services to just about any country without ever leaving my home.

That's just in labor markets, places that were harder to integrate than ever before. In other places, in other markets that are critical to our livelihoods, you might even say that global markets are almost perfectly connected, perfectly integrated, or shall we say they might just be one big market, no longer separated by an ideology, a political fence, a wall, a national border. What I'm talking about are financial markets—the Wall Streets, the markets in Shanghai, the FTSE, and the DAX. All the markets around the world are just one big financial market. Buying and selling assets across borders—that's the definition of financial markets. It's one big pool and they operate absolutely seamlessly. In financial markets, the fates of individuals, of savers and investors in one country and another, are really perfectly connected, so much so that national identity almost doesn't matter at all. It almost doesn't even enter the equation or the thinking. What happens in one financial market is exactly what matters and happens almost automatically in the other, and it happens almost instantaneously.

Maybe even more importantly, financial markets are absolutely enormous. The flow of the value of monies around the world from savers to investors, from folks in China to people in the United States, from savers in India to developers and construction workers in Rio de Janeiro is absolutely enormous. It dwarfs all other markets, and it happens so rapidly and so seamlessly that we don't even really notice it when it's happening. It's just part of the background and the framework. Those national identities really don't matter at all, and they don't even rise to the level of being something we're conscious of.

Financial markets being literally instantaneous, being so huge and enormous, have an enormous impact on the way that we live. They matter for the determination of the cost of borrowing around the world. It doesn't matter how much savings has taken place in the United States; if I want to borrow in the United States what matters is how much saving is taking place around the world. Even if no one in the United States saves anything, it might not matter. Savings might still be easy to come by, cheap to borrow, and that's because there really isn't a national market for saving. There's a world market, and it's so connected, it's so integrated, it's such a big one market, that there's no need to think about national identity at all.

This can be a good thing actually. It can be actually a very helpful thing. Having integrated highly connected markets, having one giant pool of savings and investment, can mean that people can earn more money from their wealth, earn more money by saving, and they can borrow at lower cost. It's a giant win-win, at least in some ways. Even at the beginning of the 20th century, people from around the world had the opportunity to invest around the world. There really weren't as many national boundaries, political boundaries, as many laws that prevented flows of money across borders.

But that's true again today. It permits us to venture our wealth in the emerging markets of the world, the places where we expect the highest return. It also means that if you live in an emerging market or maybe an unstable economy, you don't have to suffer all the consequences of having all your money tied up there. You can balance it out. You can spread around and have a portfolio that's balanced by really stable investments and the economies of the West or the United States or Switzerland, with money that you're willing to venture on high-growth, high-potential emerging markets in Asia and around the world. It may be a little less stable, but it's a lot more exciting and fun, and it actually generates a lot more opportunities for virtually everyone.

These types of activities have always been beneficial to savers and investors to some degree, but they come at great costs. At the beginning of the 20th century, as I already mentioned, the flows of savings were a little more liberal than they were in the middle of the 20th century. We backed away from an integrated market precisely because the costs seemed to be too high. We thought of that as a permanent situation, that once we opened the door to the venture of wealth around the world those doors would never close again, but they did. Yet they're open again, and we should ask, does it matter?

What does it all mean, living in a very flat world, the most flat in some sense that the world has ever been? It does mean that our decisions depend on the actions and even the feelings of people in other countries. We're a bit more exposed, a bit more open. There's a cost and a benefit here. Our faiths are connected to one another just as our economies are connected to one another. It doesn't matter our starting point; it doesn't matter that we're rich or that we're poor. Our competition is now virtually everyone, and that brings exciting things and some scary things too.

In the extreme, we could think about a perfectly integrated world. We're not there yet, but we're much more like one big economy than we ever have been. That's not to say that distance doesn't still matter. It's true that maybe people who compete in one country compete more so with folks in their local communities, their states, and their regions than they do with people around the world, but there's more competition. You still have to cross oceans for most goods. You still have to get on a plane to travel mostly around the world. And so distance does matter, but that distance is getting less difficult and matters less than ever before. In fact, most economies are so integrated with each other, they're so much a part of the world economy, that about a third of their jobs would have to be replaced if they went backwards and shut themselves off from the rest of the world. That's true in the United States. At least a third of our jobs are in some way deeply connected to investors and savers and producers around the world. In some ways, we're even more connected to them than we are to people who live next door.

We can formally think about this question: How connected are we? How much of a one-world economy do we actually live in? Economists do formally think about this question and always have. We can even measure it. We use something called the balance of payments. The balance of payments is just a simple accounting system. It measures the flows of resources from one economy into another, and it aggregates them across the world so that they actually balance at the end of the day. After all, what I export, someone else somewhere imports. By accounting for those flows on both the exporting end and the importing end, we understand just how much integration takes place. It's not just goods and services that we measure in the balance of payments. We also measure flows of financial funds, the flows of savings from one country to another, the demands for investment from one country to another. All of this is summarized in the balance of payments. It's the summary of any individual nation's economic relationship with the rest of the world. When we examine it, we not only know how integrated we are, we also know a little bit about what risks are out there and waiting for us.

We can think about the various components of the balance of payments. It's not the most thrilling discussion, but we can at least break it down into areas that help us understand the world a little bit better and understand how our fates are connected. One of the most basic elements of the balance of payments, something you'll see reported on virtually every week in the *Wall Street Journal*, the *Financial Times*, or some other major business periodical, is talk about the trade deficit or the trade account, how much we're exporting versus how much others are importing our goods and vice versa. In the balance of payments, this is summarized in an account called the current account, these things that are traded immediately, these one-shot transactions—you give me goods, I give you money. In the current account, we stuff all the transactions between countries for goods and services. We also trade the short-term income flows from assets like the dividend payment I get on stock that I hold in Shanghai or the interest payment I make on a loan I took out in Switzerland. But, for the most part, this is trade in goods and services that we're talking about.

The current account tells us a little bit about things we worry about. Are we competitive manufactures, or are we exporting most of our jobs overseas? Where's the future of world production, the workshop of the world, and where is it leading? But, perhaps the most important element of the balance of payments isn't really the current account, but its counterbalancing force, the capital and financial accounts. The capital and financial accounts don't tell us about goods and services flows; they tell us about flows of financial resources. All the stocks and the bonds that are traded around the world, that go from hedge fund investors in one country to another, for good or for bad, well that's in the capital and financial account. By watching that, we can examine part of the history of the world and how it unfolds, and the risks that are taking place and being shared are sometimes even spread around the world.

It's also the place where we look for some signs of economic management and mismanagement within countries. In the capital, the financial accounts will get some sense of official reserves and the stock of monies that countries might use to protect themselves should the weather turn harsh, should they need to defend their currency against overnight capital flows. When we look at the combination of the capital account and the current account, we see a little bit about the story of how the world is unfolding and certainly about how integration matters.

One of the most clear ways and one of the clearest stories we can see about how integrated we are with the rest of the world, how much of a single world economy we live in, is to examine some of the activities amongst the world's largest economies. I can think of no better example than of the United States and China throughout most of the end of the 20th century and certainly the beginning of the 21st. A lot of anxiety surrounds the discussion of how we're connected to China and how China is connected to us and about how our fates are really deeply intertwined. In fact, one might say that what the Chinese do is even more important to the United States than what a lot of U.S. states do to each other and with each other. That story of integration and being connected is key to understanding how much connectedness really matters.

There's a shorthand for it. We know a little bit about the story already. In particular in that relationship between the United States and China, we know that in the United States, a consumer-heavy country, we buy lots of goods and services that are produced in China, mostly goods. We also know that conversely we have a large trade deficit, which means that we buy lots of exports of goods from the rest of the world, but not that many people buy ours—or at least relative to our imports, our exports of goods and services are relatively modest. There's a question in there that you may not pick up on, but if we're sending all these dollars out into the world to buy the goods and services of the rest of the world and the rest of the world doesn't really need all those dollars to buy our goods and services, what are they doing with the rest of the money?

That's an important question; I'll say it again. When we send hundreds of billions of dollars out into the world, and the world doesn't need them to buy things back from us, what do they do with that excess cash? Why does someone in some foreign exchange market even take it? Why do they receive those dollars and accept them? The short answer is that if you only look at goods and services trade, there is a deficit, but what you don't look at is the entire picture. Sure they're receiving excess dollars, and sure they don't need those dollars to buy our goods, our cars, our toasters, our toys. What they do with those dollars is buy other things that we sell like our assets, those assets in the capital and financial accounts. They buy things like stocks and bonds and companies and land. That means very important things for the citizens of the United States. It means that we get lower interest rates. After all, there are more people willing to invest and send financial resources back to us.

It also means that we get higher asset values. In that act of buying our assets, buying our property and our stocks and bonds, we get higher asset values. Our fates and some of the things that we care the most about, the value in our 401(k)'s, the value in our properties, in some sense they're much more determined by actions in China than they are by people who act right here in the United States. That's important because if we believe we live in a world where this type of imbalance can't last forever, where we can't over import and under export forever, we'll have to rebalance. We'll have to move back to a world where we do more exporting than before, and the Chinese buy fewer and fewer of our assets. That means that there will be less supporting those asset values, and so they're likely to fall, or that we'll have to find a way to move people into export jobs. It matters a lot for the shape, color, and character of our economy. How much is that? How much does it really matter? Well, an awful lot. It means that interconnectedness really matters an awful lot.

Think about it this way—some things that are really personal, the mortgage rate that you pay on your home, the rate that you buy your car with, the job that you hold, where you work, and certainly how much you get paid all heavily depends on actions that take place completely outside the United States, by people who don't live under your same laws and your same culture. That's a bit interesting, maybe disquieting, but it also offers lots of opportunities. It's not just in the United States that things are cheaper and borrowing is cheaper, but in China you get things too. After all, the ability to export in such large volumes to the United States means they can create an awful lot of manufacturing jobs year in and year out. With the creation of those jobs and the higher incomes that come along with them, they create a better life, a better world, and hope for the people in rural communities who moved to the coast to get those jobs. In short, they create a lot of political stability that's necessary to maintain the balance in this giant rapidly growing economy that's key to the 21st century. We get a lot out of being connected, and so do a lot of other countries too.

But, there's the risk that goes along with it. Never is there an economic story, it seems, where there is all good and no bad. There's a downside, or at least some risks we must attend to and understand to really handle integration in a formal way. For example, integration means that a problem, a financial hiccup in one part of the world, will be immediately felt in another. That's because financial markets are large, perfectly integrated practically, and instantaneously connected. One problem in one distant land is automatically acted upon and reacted upon around the world with great consequence.

In fact, one of the most important stories of the last decade of the 20th century was the story of the Asian Financial Crisis. This was a great story of super powerful economic behemoths really changing their minds about small rapidly growing Asian Tigers. The story of the Asian Financial Crisis is a story of a little hiccup that became a bigger hiccup in Thailand. Suddenly, with that hiccup, financial flows began to race out of the region—and not just Thailand, but all the other financial Tiger economies of that region. With that rapid flow out of those economies, those economies had to react quickly, and some of them were toppled. The devastation that ensued was equivalent [to, or] like, the Great Depression in the United States. It was all the result of this integration that many up to that point had believed would only be for the good. We learned then how integration can raise the stakes in a global economy. In raising the stakes, it raises the demands on us too.

One of the best things about living in a world that's deeply integrated, where financial markets are really part of one giant market, where goods and labor markets are connected around the world, is that any producer, any competitive firm, has an opportunity to benefit by selling into a much bigger market. That's a wonderful thing. Maybe you build the best mousetrap, maybe you build the best cars, and you're not just limited to selling it to individuals in your region, state, or country, but around the world. The upside is extraordinary. Maybe you make the best movies, and you can sell them not just in the United States, but around the world. The financial benefits of that are extraordinary.

Not only that, but if you want to take a chance, become an entrepreneur, you have access to much cheaper finance, because we live in a world that's financially integrated. You don't just depend on savers around the corner or even your rich uncle, you depend on the whole savings of the world. That can be everything to an entrepreneur—cheap finance, the availability of money to get started and stay going when times are tough, can make the difference between success and failure. But, the costs are connections to competitors around the world—other individuals, other entrepreneurs, other movie markers, and other competitive multinational firms. That can be good for consumers, but it's awfully difficult to manage. The stakes are higher, and so are the potential rewards.

We can't even say that, in a globally integrated world, to citizens of the United States, we can think a New Yorker has as much connection to someone in

Beijing financially and economically as they may to an individual who lives in California. Sure, Beijing probably matters as much to a New Yorker or maybe Toronto matters even more to a New Yorker than some who live in the United States. It doesn't mean that they're more important to us in a social sense. But in a financial and economic sense, that's exactly what it means. That raises a complex set of questions about the world that we want to live in and how our societies are constructed. If there are no borders between economies, should there be borders politically? Should we have the same laws and culture? These are tensions that are ever present, and the stakes of them are raised in a financially integrated global economy. We live in an integrated world, and the world is also a more complex world. It's not necessarily a bad thing; it's just really different.

In closing, we could say that there's no doubt that all of the efforts of the 20th century to knock down walls, to reduce barriers, to take growth where it never was before, and to take opportunity, democracy, and different cultures and different ideas to where they never were before has really integrated the planet. Coupled with technology that's made distance almost irrelevant, certainly for some things, we live in a world that's really much more like one giant economy than ever before. This more integrated, more connected flatter world, offers us a world of benefits—some that were unimaginable. But, it asks an awful lot of us too. To that we can never stop adapting. We must learn much, much more about an integrated world to live peacefully in it, and to prosper as we've done in previous decades.

# China's Policies and the World Economy
## Lecture 12

> … China is almost certainly the future of the world economy; at a billion plus people, growing at 8 or 9 or 10 percent per year—and already the second largest economy in the world—they'd almost have to be.

As we've discussed, no country has the potential to affect the world economy as much as China does, although at the time of the Great Leap Forward, just a few decades ago, the Chinese made some disastrous mistakes. Then, Deng Xiaoping realized that the nation had to break away from the command economy and begin to adopt free-market ideas. As he said, "It doesn't matter what color a cat is as long as it catches mice." In other words, the particular ideology of change wasn't as important as the change itself.

Deng started his experimentation rather modestly, by allowing farmers to keep their own excess production. Almost immediately, there began a period of much higher agricultural productivity and, with it, the birth of real markets. The situation was similar to how the Industrial Revolution began in Western Europe. Next came the need for more infrastructure to bring these markets together, and the Chinese government responded. The population grew excited; people began to invest in themselves and to offer political support to the idea that opening up could lead to a rebirth of the Chinese economy.

Despite these changes, at the beginning of the 1980s, China was still profoundly poor, but then the nation began to grow rapidly. It did so through investment in infrastructure, education, and technology. Further, wages in China were so low that Chinese products were attractive to consumers around the world.

By keeping their currency relatively cheap, the Chinese also ensured that their production was attractive and that new exports could come from China to service the rest of the world. This strategy led to the birth of jobs and manufacturing in China on a scale that solidified the buy-in and ensured further economic growth. After about the mid-1980s, Chinese growth averaged more than 8 percent per year. Throughout this process, China moved into the position of uncontested factory of the world, and prices for manufactured goods plummeted.

Global capital began to flow into China to create manufacturing facilities there. At the same time, the Chinese were using the excess income they received to buy other currencies, increasing the demand for dollars or euros, increasing the supply of renminbi or yuan, and keeping Chinese wages low in foreign currency terms. This had a significant impact on the world economy. Manufacturing in the West or in middle-income countries couldn't compete with China. Further, this economic growth in China had the potential to affect the environment, sovereignty around the world, quality of life in the workplace, and many other aspects of life. It's also important to note that China's growth lifted hundreds of millions of people out of poverty.

**Investment is so critical. It's really the key to growth because investment is the key to productivity, and productivity is the key to growth.**

By the middle of the 21st century, China could easily be significantly larger than any other economy in the world. It's already the global center of production, but will it be the center of finance? The Chinese Communist Party still holds a good deal of control and still restricts capital flows, which won't allow the nation to become a banking center. But if the Chinese gradually become more open, it makes sense the China will become the economic center of the world. ∎

## Suggested Reading

Bhagwati, *In Defense of Globalization.*
Helpman, *The Mystery of Economic Growth.*

1.  What are the similarities between China's economic success and that of the West during the Industrial Revolution? Are the fundamentals of growth the same for both examples?

2.  What will China need to do to sustain high growth rates?

# China's Policies and the World Economy
## Lecture 12—Transcript

Welcome back. Thus far throughout the course we've done an awful lot of study of the economic history of the world. We've looked at some of the best stories, the miracles as I've called them—the Western economic miracle, the miracle in Japan, and the astounding success of the Asian Tigers. Maybe it's time we actually stop looking back and try to think a little bit about looking forward. Let's ask ourselves what's the U.S. economy going to look like in the coming century? What's the world economy going to look like in the coming century? If we want you to do that, if we want to really think about what's going to happen in the coming century, we need to think about what countries have the most potential to change things, about what countries and what policies and what regions will be the most influential in determining the fates of our economies and the status of our economic lives in the 21st century and beyond.

If we want to do that, then we have to really start with China. I would say that no country anywhere has the potential to affect the world economy nearly as much as does China. To some degree you could say without too much exaggeration that it really is the future of the world economy, or at least it has to be more of it than any other country. There's no other economy that has the potential to do what China will do to the 21st century. In fact, I would say no country in history seems to have more potential to affect world economic output than does this one.

It makes us wonder why China wasn't sort of on the map so much sooner. We wonder how they went from being so large and supreme to so insignificant and then started all the way back again. We can start to learn that by thinking back to where they were just a couple of decades ago. You recall in a previous lecture I talked about how I remembered mothers and grandmothers sitting at the table saying finish your supper, don't you know there's starving children in China. They said to be grateful for that food and it was literally true. That disaster, that failure of the second 5-year plan, actually started pretty well, but it tells us a little bit about the source of economic growth in China, their missteps, and how they eventually took the right course.

That second 5-year plan that's now called the Great Leap Forward was represented by a couple of things that were really tragic mistakes. One of the mistakes was that they had taken farmers who had farmed the land for generations and understood the land well and tried to get them to impose different techniques, dig deeper in the soil when they knew that that was a bad idea or plant crops really close together when no one had ever done that before. They changed the plans of the experts and, in so doing, they brought about economic disaster. Not only that, they did something maybe even worse. They asked the specialists in farming to become steelmakers and iron makers and diverted them from all the activities they knew and could command to do very well. The result was absolutely disastrous. It was really a model of misdirection. They took this great asset, these people who knew everything about doing the most important thing you can do first in an economy—and that's to feed people—and they made them become something completely different. They took away their skills, they took away their own plans, and they forced them to divert their activity. They went from doing something at which they were very productive to trying to do something else, make steel and iron, at which they were not very productive at all.

On top of that, they also had a few terrible meteorological disasters. The Yellow River flooded, and it was a flood for a generation. There was a drought that followed. So terrible, so awful was this period of the Great Leap Forward in terms of agricultural output, the grain production in 1960 was only 30% of grain production in 1958. It absolutely devastated this very poor economy.

A couple of years back, I remember looking back on all those images of the Tiananmen Square protests. Those images are vivid in my mind. I remember seeing them at the time, and I certainly remember that wonderful image of the young man standing in front of the tank. I remembered also seeing the standard signs of protest. There were people raising signs, yelling and screaming, marching, and there were a certain group of people who were starving themselves and telling the media that they intended to starve themselves until the changes were made. It didn't strike me at the time. Certainly that's a profound thing, but it didn't resonate with me in the way that it should have because I wasn't Chinese. Until I talked to a Chinese colleague who told me how powerful that was for a Chinese individual to voluntarily go without food, to starve themselves, and to hearken back to all the misery and disaster that had been present in that economy was to really remind everyone of just how serious they were about these changes and how important they were. It reminds us that in China this economy we now think of as so fantastic and stellar, starvation and the absolute disasters of economic failure were once so present that they still hold a central place in the Chinese cultural identity.

Just a couple of decades earlier in the 1970s, China had actually become smaller than ever in the world economy. It had become so small as to become almost insignificant. This was an economy really beset with massive poverty. In terms of the world economy, it was shut off. It was something else. It was completely off the map. It wasn't just the Second World or the Third World; it was practically another planet. Then something actually began to change. It became obvious to at least one person, Deng Xiaoping—who had become the premiere at that time—it had become obvious to him that China had to change course. He had a wonderful way of thinking about that. They had to move from being a command economy with plans so centralized and so specific that they limited all entrepreneurial activity, that they prevented others and the individual people throughout the economy for making their own choices about business. They had to break away from that and do something that was really radical. They had to start to adopt kind of free-market ideas. They had to move toward the model of the West, something that would've been detested and heavily resisted earlier, but he had to make this happen.

He had a very practical way of looking at the world, and he said something that really resonated throughout the ages. He's noted for having said at this time "It doesn't matter what color a cat is, as long as it catches mice." That's a very nice way to summarize this change. It didn't matter that an ideology or an ism was needed to make a change, that China was going to change course in a dramatic fashion. What they needed was an economic plan that got the job done, that fed people. It all started rather modestly actually, a little bit of production around the edges. There was an experimentation period where Deng actually asked farmers to keep their own excess production. Everyone had a quota to provide to the state, and that was a very limiting quota. It was

181

something that was a very serious event. If you didn't provide the quota, there could be serious penalties. Most of what farmers did was work as hard as they could to actually meet the quota. Anything they produced over the quota also went back to the state. In a simple change, Deng said let them keep any excess production that they have, let that be theirs, and therefore let that motivate them to actually produce the quota as quickly as possible, so that they could get to the point where they were actually producing goods for themselves to keep and to use as they chose for whatever they chose.

Almost immediately there began a period of much higher agricultural productivity—surprise, surprise. What a wonderful thing, that small change, that incentive—not a radical overnight shock therapy [to] reinvent the economy, just change something at the margin, experiment, and that's precisely what Deng did. It worked famously well. Farmers began to work in more difficult soils. They began to expand their production. They did everything they could to make sure that they had something to trade for themselves, and that was really the beginning of a free-market revolution in China. Think about what happens next. You have a little bit of excess production, you have a little bit more food than you needed, and perhaps then you can take that food and begin to trade it. You can begin to use it for other things. Maybe you have enough excess production of wheat or rice, and you could trade that for an oven, a washing machine, maybe a bicycle, something simple. But it was the real birth of a market, the way markets are more or less always born. People have production that's in excess of what they need to survive and they trade it. They trade it to others. As they trade it, they begin to create markets, for new goods and new services. That was really the birth, this agricultural revolution.

It's interesting to think about it in those terms because, in some ways, it's really similar to how the Industrial Revolution began in Western Europe and England. First, there was an agricultural revolution. Without agricultural production sufficient to sustain the population, you really can't do anything else. An economy may be very hungry, and when it's very hungry it needs food. It doesn't need iPods and computers and automobiles. The first thing you have to do is feed the people, and this change, this modest incentive change, did just that. It birthed the rest of the markets that suddenly started to grow around it.

182

It was a modest beginning that led to a much less modest middle part, this middle period when there was lots of excess production of agriculture, and people needed not just more food, but more of everything else. Suddenly there was a demand for more of everything—more merchants, more specialists, more production, and more than just China could produce. They needed it from everywhere else. If they needed all this production and the forces to bring markets together, they also needed a lot of government investment in infrastructure. That's just what they got.

Along with that buy-in and that investment in infrastructure, they got a population that was really excited for the first time in a long time. There was this beginning of a distance between economic disaster, between literal starvation and the way people lived day in and day out, that they could believe in this system. They could buy the idea that changing course, moving from a cat of one color to a cat of another color, was actually a really good idea. They began to invest more in themselves and offer much more political support to the idea that opening up could lead to a full rebirth of the Chinese economy, could help it ascend back to its natural place at the top of the world economy. This buy-in, this critical early win and early victories, these actually set the stage for a wonderful period of Chinese growth. That buy-in was achieved through these small changes in the same way that buy-ins in other plans and other schemes for growth have taken place in other countries. The early wins mattered an awful lot.

But, it wasn't just early wins that made things work. Sure, you can have a little bit of agricultural production, but China in the beginning in the early part of the 1980s was still really profoundly poor. But, then they began to grow at really rapid rates and one began to wonder how were they doing it. What is the Chinese story? Is it really a different one? Certainly, we hadn't seen this quite before, a fully communist closed-off economy, a giant suddenly becoming huge and rich seemingly overnight, growing at rapid rates. The truth of it was the fundamentals were not that difficult. What the Chinese economy did to grow really wasn't all that different than what other economies had done to grow.

To begin, they had a lot of investment. Investment is so critical. It's really the key to growth because investment is the key to productivity, and productivity is the key to growth. What the Chinese economy did was generate some excess resources and not consume them, but pour them back into the economy itself, pour it back into roads and ports, pour it back into people and training, and pour it back into technologies that helped them all become more productive. In so doing they set the stage for further growth. More than that, they also began to enter the world economy when their wages were very, very low relative to any peer workers around the world. Their wages were so low that the products they could produce, whatever quality they were—and they actually began pretty good—would be attractive to consumers all around the world. That was another key to the fundamentals, a simple strategy that works time and time again. They also just loosened up, and they gave workers more freedom to move wherever the market drew them. The market was drawing workers from the countryside to the coastal cities where trading and entrepreneurial activity were just bursting at the seams. Allowing that freedom for the first time meant that they allowed the free markets to work their magic in a place where they had been completely banned before.

There were a lot of elements. It's actually not a short story, it's a long one, but there were some key elements that deserve a little more attention. One of them that comes up time and time again is what the Chinese did with regard to their currency. What they did with regard to their currency is actually really important. One of the ways that they remained relevant to the world and really opened up as the workshop for the world is that they ensured that Chinese production was cheap and value-rich for consumers around the world. They made sure that Chinese products were relatively cheap. You might think to yourself, how would you do that? Do you force wages to be low? Do you force your firms to accept very low profits? You might think of all these things, but there's actually a simpler way to do that. All you need to do is to make sure that your currency is cheap relative to other currencies. Make sure that one dollar buys an awful lot of yuan or renminbi, so that it can therefore buy a lot of Chinese production, a lot of Chinese workers' time and energy, and a lot of Chinese factory time and energy. They made sure that on the macroeconomic front, they printed, injected into the system, an awful lot of their own currency to keep it low cost, to make sure that prices were low in China. It's almost like a commercial strategy you would think about at a private business. By keeping their currency relatively cheap, they ensured that Chinese production was relatively attractive and that new exports could come from China to service the rest of the world. That led to the birth of jobs and manufacturing in China on a scale that solidified the buy-in and ensured further economic growth.

Growth actually was really rapid. The Chinese economy after Deng's vision in 1978 that he had to make a change, of course, was remarkable. They begin to grow at a rate of 7–10% per year easily. It's actually a little hard to even get good statistics. That's in some sense how weak the economy was at the beginning. But before long, by about the middle of the 1980s, Chinese income levels had already doubled. That's remarkable; 7 or 8 years to double your per capita income. It's happened before, and I've mentioned it before, but you should really try to imagine that. Imagine the first doubling of your income from absolute poverty to something else and how that must feel, how that must transform a culture almost overnight.

Think about it in more concrete terms. Chinese income levels went from about $1 per day to about $2 per day. In most rich economies that doesn't sound like much at all, but it's a night and day difference. Imagine what that marginal dollar per day really meant to you, how it meant a difference in what you could have. You could have for the first time something, some excess, a new set of anything—second pair of shoes, an oven, something beyond simply scrimping by. You could afford also to think about the future, to dream about a better time and a better place. What an optimistic time that would have been. It wasn't just your income that was doubling; it was everyone's. In that there was an optimism and a sense of purpose and a sense of destiny that revisited China.

After the mid-1980s, that economy embarked upon a pace of growth that was wonderful and huge internally, but still relatively modest in terms of its impact on the rest of the world. Think about the math really simply: $400 extra per person times 1 billion people, that's $400 billion more of world GDP. Actually, that's really just a drop in the bucket. While the world watched and was awed and while Chinese people were amazed, the world didn't really feel that in a heavy way, but that would come soon enough, because soon enough the Chinese economy embarked upon a world leading pace of growth. Really, it was something remarkable. It's true that that story of Japan and its remarkable ascendance and of the Asian Tigers and their remarkable ascendance seemed to be repeating itself in another Asian economy in China. For the next 25-plus years, Chinese economic growth averaged more than 8% per year. Even in real per capita terms, even looking at the apples-to-apples comparisons of how much income an individual had year in and year out, they were growing at an incredible pace. There was no end in sight; the momentum was absolutely remarkable.

Throughout the process, they moved from being a serious competitor, a second place to manufacture, the place to manufacture for all Asian economies, to being the legitimate, genuine, and uncontested factory of the world. Manufactured goods virtually seemed to all come from China. They had a huge impact on the price of goods around the world. Short answer is they plummeted. Manufactured goods, everything from televisions to toys to automobiles and their components, plummeted in price around the world in inflation-adjusted terms because the Chinese could produce more and more year in and year out at cheaper and cheaper prices. That had a remarkable effect not only on consumers around the world, but on producers around the world who suddenly figured either they had to find some special way to compete with low wages and prices in China or go there themselves. That's more or less precisely what they did.

Global capital began to flow into China in a remarkable way. We'd think of this as direct investment or foreign direct investment, flows of money from around the world to create manufacturing facilities in China. That's a huge part of this story. But, on the other hand, the Chinese were also exporting a lot of capital. Not only were they receiving a lot of money from around the world, they were also sending a lot of it back. In fact, they were sending a lot of it back to the United States. This connection isn't always easy to make, but this is part of the way they helped keep their currency cheap to create this whole system of low wages, lots of manufacturing production, and growth.

It works like this: By selling a lot of goods and services to the world, they receive a lot of the world's income, just like the United States sends a lot of money to China to buy their goods and services. The Chinese then take that money, they use some of it for their own imports, but they send the rest back out, buying those other currencies. Maybe they want to buy treasury bills, and so what do they do? They trade their currency for dollars. Maybe they want to buy bonds in Europe and they trade their currency for euros. In either case, what they're doing is increasing the demand for dollars or euros and increasing the supply of renminbi, yuan. They're increasing that supply making that price cheaper and cheaper and sending capital throughout the world. It works its magic throughout the world buying up assets and raising prices, and it also works its magic by keeping Chinese wages relatively low in foreign currency terms. To holders of dollars and holders of euros, that process keeps Chinese manufacturing output cheap. That's what keeps China in business to a large degree.

It was really this basic process of a relatively inexpensive Chinese currency and therefore relatively inexpensive Chinese output and wages that meant the world was in for a big surprise. This had a huge impact on the world economy. It meant that manufacturing around the world really began to shift in a big way and stable industries became unhinged. Manufacturing jobs that could reside in the West, that could reside in not only high income, but even middle-income countries, really found they couldn't compete with China at all. China was actually swallowing up the rest of the world in a way that did have a big impact. Suddenly they were not only big enough, but rich enough to really impact the world.

It forced everybody to stop and think. What a wonderful story it is to see China growing at the pace of Japan or the Asian Tigers, but there's a really key difference. Singapore is tiny, Taiwan is tiny, Hong Kong is tiny—all those economies are small relative to China. Even a big one like Japan at about 100 million people is only one-tenth the size of China. China at 4 times the population of the United States, and still growing, might have an extraordinary impact on the world. Was the world ready for that? There could have been a lot of impacts, and we need to think about all of them—impacts on pollution, impacts on the stability of jobs around the world, impacts on sovereignty, and impacts on quality of life in the workplace around so many parts of the world. But, there are good things, too. One of the most important things that came out of the Chinese growth story was the alleviation of poverty. When we talk about their numbers and we talk about their incomes going from $1 a day to $2 a day, what we're really saying is that economic miracle lifted hundreds of millions of people from the brink of economic insignificance. They lifted them out of poverty. In fact, if you want to look at the reduction in poverty around the world since 1975, the vast majority of it has occurred in China. Four hundred million people were easily lifted from that threshold of abject poverty of $1 a day. That's an extraordinarily successful program. I'd be hard pressed to think of any aid program from the United States, European Union, or the World Bank that even nearly approximated that level of success, but that's what the Chinese were embarked upon, and it was still taking place.

It meant for the first time that poverty, which had been really an Asian problem, became de-Asianized. This was the beginning of a move from poverty being defined by Indians and Chinese to really being defined by Africans. The move of Chinese economy over that period really meant that poverty changed in a fundamental way. It was being eradicated from one place. You might think if I had a magic wand, and I could choose one country I wanted to grow quickly, you probably would have chosen China because you would've had the largest effect on real poverty and suffering around the world. It's amazing that we have this story of global poverty reduction in an economy that, on the one hand, is very poor and still weak and, on the other hand, is even the largest source of global capital flows. It's so big that it has these differential effects. It can be poor and still really powerful or have low incomes and still have an enormous impact on the world. That's really the first time that's happened in hundreds and hundreds of years.

You might think that's ironic, that you could have a large population of an economy that's also poor or a poor economy that was also powerful. But, really, it's just part and parcel of what it meant to be China, this huge economy that was growing rich. The money that they were earning wasn't staying in China—some of it was, but the rest was flowing out. Not only were they a source of the world's demand for products, they were a source of the world's finances. They were taking their place being important in lots of different ways. They were highly significant to the world, and it's very important that they remain that way because as a large economy if they didn't remain that way, the rest of the world would feel the jolt.

For that reason we can say that China is almost certainly the future of the world economy at a billion plus people growing at 8 or 9 or 10% per year—and, already the second largest economy in the world, they'd almost have to be. We can engage in a few thought experiments that help us round that out. Just imagine if China keeps it up for a little while longer. Maybe another decade of growth where they are that instead of doubling their incomes from $400 per person to $800, they'll be doubling them from $3,000–$4,000 to $8,000. Suddenly you're talking big numbers—$4 or $5 trillion of incremental world GDP per year. That's an enormous impact, an enormous strain on physical resources, but also an enormous amount of profit, an enormous amount of production for the world to share, and perhaps an enormous amount of better living in China.

As the largest economy of the world, and by a long shot, it's going to be there. It'll be the largest economy very soon. One would predict that by at least the middle of the 21st century, China will be so much larger than most other economies that it'll be more or less uncontested. That's certainly possible. Already one could say it's the center of production around the world—or at least if there is a center, that's probably it. But, is it going to be the center of the world economy as a whole? One question that remains is whether or not it will be the center of world finance. That's a more difficult trick for anyone to pull. Already it's a great source of capital flows, but it's an economy that really isn't open to the inward flow and outward flow. The Chinese Communist Party still holds a good deal of control and still restricts capital flows, and that just doesn't work if you want to be a banking center. But, if they change that as well, if they engage in gradual opening year in and year out, it probably makes more sense than any other location.

When I think back about China and their growth and their astounding change from being remarkably poor to being set on the path to literally changing the shape of the world economy, I think this is amazing. For 150 years or more, the secrets of the Industrial Revolution just didn't leak into China in any way. But, when they finally leaked in, when they finally began to emerge through some simple ideas and changes around the margin, it absolutely worked its magic just as it did hundreds of years ago in the economies of Western Europe. It says that China, who went from losing its historical position at the beginning of that revolution to probably getting it back, is going to have gone through this whole course and prove that everything can happen. An economy that's wonderful can become tragic and a cautionary tale and can return from that fate to become something amazing and quite different.

When we think about China, we think is this growth really possible? Is it really sustainable around the world? Can we live with this level of growth? There are no real sharp answers to that. Certainly China and its growth, given its size, will force us to consider what it really means to live in a world where the largest economy by population also is struggling to become one of the most rich, one of the most powerful, one of the economies with the highest income. The world could relatively easily make room and shape for a country like Singapore or for Taiwan or for even other small economies around the world, but can it make room for China? We hope that it can, but that presents new challenges that are difficult to confront and completely unknown at this point.

We might think in closing that China offers us a lot of lessons. It does offer a lot of lessons; some of them are the standard ones. To grow you need buy-in from the population. You need to let the free market have at least some of its sway. You need to have a way to make average workers more productive year in and year out. That means investing in them, saving enough or drawing enough from around the world to invest in their training, in an infrastructure, and in an environment that benefits all productive activities.

Perhaps it also teaches us something about how economies fail. If you think about it, the Chinese economy and its failure tell us a little bit about the power of ideas. What could've possibly held back that economy with all of its riches, with all of its cultural history, with all of the resources it had, to topple the giant and make it a Lilliputian over a period of a few hundred years? That's just the power of ideas. If you ever question how powerful they are, all you have to do is look at the Chinese economy. Good ideas could help that economy go from insignificance and being beset with abject poverty to being rich, but they could also do the reverse. Maybe what Chinese economic history really teaches us is that bad ideas are really powerful. They're so powerful that, well, they're more powerful than even the biggest of giants.

# Glossary

**absolute advantage**: A concept originated by Adam Smith. If one economy can produce more of a product than another using the same amount of resources, the higher producer is said to have an absolute advantage over the lower producer. In this situation, it is beneficial for the two producers to engage in trade of the products that give them an absolute advantage.

**average worker productivity**: Calculated by dividing total economic output (GDP) by the number of employed workers in an economy.

**balance of payments**: An accounting system that measures the flows of resources from one economy into another and aggregates them across the world. Provides a summary of an individual nation's economic relationship with the rest of the world.

**bubble**: Rapid expansion of an economy, followed by an often-dramatic contraction.

**capital account**: One component of the balance of payments; provides information about financial flows in an economy.

**capitalism**: A free-market economic system characterized by private ownership of property and goods.

**command economy**: An economy in which the central government makes all relevant economic decisions.

**comparative advantage**: An extension of Adam Smith's concept of absolute advantage, developed by David Ricardo. The idea that even in a situation of absolute advantage, trade is still beneficial between two economies if the lower-producing economy specializes in some aspect of production.

**corruption**: The abuse of power for private gain.

**current account**: One component of the balance of payments; provides information about the flow of goods and services in an economy.

**deflation**: A situation of falling prices for goods and services.

**free market**: A system in which business is conducted according to the laws of supply and demand, without government intervention. Participants in free markets reap all the benefits and incur all the costs of their actions.

**gray market**: Trade that falls outside of normal distribution channels. Gray-market trade can often be found in developing economies, where sellers with no connection to the original manufacturer offer for sale such items as electronics and DVDs at discounted prices.

**gross domestic product (GDP)**: A measure of a nation's economic activity; the total value of all goods and services produced in an economy in a given year.

**hegemony**: Economic or other influence exerted by a dominant nation.

**hyperinflation**: Inflation that grows at a very high rate in a short time period.

**inflation**: A situation of rising prices for goods and services.

**law of demand**: With all other factors equal, the demand for a product will decrease as its price increases.

**law of one price**: The idea that one product should never have two particular prices in one market.

**leverage**: The use of credit to enhance an investor's ability to make additional investments.

**liquidity**: The ability to quickly realize the value of an asset; the ease with which an asset may be exchanged for cash.

**macroeconomics**: A branch of economics concerned with the study of economic systems as a whole.

**microeconomics**: A branch of economics concerned with the study of individual aspects of an economy, such as firms or prices.

**misery index**: A measure developed in the 1970s to describe a poor economic state. Calculated by adding the unemployment rate to the inflation rate.

**monetarism**: School of thought in which the money supply is believed to have a significant influence on economic factors, such as inflation rates.

**opportunity cost**: The cost of an alternative that must be eliminated in making a decision. The classic example is the money a student would have earned had he or she chosen to work rather than attend college.

**per capita GDP**: GDP divided by the total population of a country.

**recession**: A period of reduced activity in an economy.

**scale production**: The ability to produce on a large as opposed to an individual scale; realized with the advent of the Industrial Revolution.

**socialism**: An economic system in which the state maintains ownership of the means of production.

**tariffs**: Duties on imports. Raising tariffs is a strategy used to diminish or prevent trade.

**theory of the second best**: Explains the state of flux that results when one option must be eliminated in a decision-making situation. Eliminating one option may mean that other variables in the decision are changed.

**Washington Consensus**: A now-controversial set of economic policy recommendations compiled from the World Bank, the U.S. Treasury, and other international financial institutions by John Williamson in 1990 and directed toward developing economies in crisis.

# Bibliography

Bastiat, Frederic. *Economic Fallacies*. La Vergne, TN: Simon Publications, 2001. A classic collection of writings on all manner of questions about political economy, protectionism, government intervention in free markets, and the virtues of good commerce.

Bhagwati, Jagdish. *In Defense of Globalization*. New York: Oxford University Press, 2004. The doyen of modern free traders offers convincing evidence of globalization's virtues and impact on poverty alleviation.

De Soto, Hernando. *The Mystery of Capital: Why Capitalism Triumphs in the West and Fails Everywhere Else*. New York: Basic Books, 2000. *The Mystery of Capital* offers a rare glimpse into a deliberate economic experiment that reveals some of the preconditions for capitalism to take root.

Diamond, Jared. *Guns, Germs and Steel: The Fates of Human Societies*. New York: W.W. Norton and Company, 1997. Diamond offers insight into the roles of technological advance, globalization, and luck in shaping the modern world.

Easterly, William Russell. *The Elusive Quest for Growth: Economists' Adventures and Misadventures in the Tropics*. Cambridge, MA: MIT Press, 2001. Easterly's gift lies in elucidating the challenges of defining good economic practice in a world that doesn't often work as theory suggests. The book offers a window into how economic policies and ideologies have fared in actuality over the past 50 years.

Faulkner, Robert, and Susan Shell, eds. *America at Risk: Threats to Liberal Self-Government in an Age of Uncertainty*. Ann Arbor, MI: University of Michigan Press, 2009. This collection of essays considers the many ways that the United States is adapting and must continue to adapt to the challenges of modernity in a global economy.

Friedman, Milton, and Anna J. Schwartz. *A Monetary History of the United States: 1867–1960*. Princeton, NJ: Princeton University Press, 1971. No other book can claim to have done a more complete job of explaining the monetary causes of the initiation and propagation of the Great Depression. It is also the defining book for monetarist thought and a prescient guide to contemporary concerns over banking and the role of financial markets in modern economies.

Friedman, Thomas. *The World Is Flat: A Brief History of the 21st Century*. New York: Farrar, Strauss and Giroux, 2005. Friedman offers a wonderful look into the anxieties and opportunities of a modern global and technologically advanced economy.

Gambetta, Diego. *The Sicilian Mafia: The Business of Private Protection*. Boston: Harvard University Press, 1993. Understanding the Sicilian Mafia in part offers an understanding of the vital needs of commercial enterprises in any economy. Gambetta's framing of the Mafia as primarily an organization that produces, sells, and at times, consumes protection from others yields insights into the critical institutions of capitalism.

Grossman, Gene M., and Elhanan Helpman. *Innovation and Growth in the Global Economy*. Cambridge, MA: MIT Press, 1993. Grossman and Helpman offer this lucid and technically sophisticated look at how global economies integrate to foster technological innovation, the essential seed of continuous growth worldwide.

Helpman, Elhanan. *The Mystery of Economic Growth*. Boston: Harvard University Press, 2004. One of the modern masters of international economics ponders the fundamental questions of growth and explains why so many of the answers remain a mystery.

Keynes, John Maynard. *The Economic Consequences of the Peace*. New York: Penguin Books, 1990. Keynes's hard look at the aftermath of World War II and the problems it created for the global economy is as powerful now as it was almost a century ago.

————. *The General Theory of Employment, Interest and Money*. New York: Prometheus Books, 1997. Keynes's magnum opus and the book that defines the great divide in modern economic thought between believers in the purity of markets and those that support some level of intentional policy. Modern macroeconomics, its terminology, and concepts did not exist prior to Keynes.

Kindleberger, Charles P. *The World in Depression*. Berkeley, CA: University of California Press, 1973. This book offers a fantastic, detailed account of the global impact of the Great Depression and how it challenged and challenges our understanding of the economy.

Krugman, Paul. *The Return of Depression Economics*. New York: W.W. Norton and Company, 2000. Nobel Prize winner Krugman revitalizes some of Keynes's better insights through an examination of how economies have continued to steer off course decades after the Great Depression.

Landes, David S. *Revolution in Time: Clocks and the Making of the Modern World*. Boston: Harvard University Press, 1993. Landes offers a powerful and deep examination into the role of technology in changing human behavior and shaping it toward an obsession with productivity.

Naim, Moises. *Illicit: How Smugglers, Traffickers, and Copycats Are Hijacking the Global Economy*. New York: Anchor Books, 2005. Naim offers a terrific and startling account of the challenges of making productivity the most profitable route to financial success.

Prahalad, C. K. *The Fortune at the Bottom of the Pyramid: Eradicating Poverty through Profits*. Philadelphia: Wharton School Publishing, 2006. By reimagining the poor, Prahalad invites a new discussion of the roles of business and globalization in the alleviation of poverty worldwide.

Rajan, Raghuram, and Luigi Zingales. *Saving Capitalism from the Capitalists: Unleashing the Power of Financial Markets to Create Wealth and Spread Opportunity*. New York: Crown Business, 2003. Rajan and Zingales synthesize much of their great work, explaining the role and value of the financial sector to any economy. The book also describes the ways in which the possibilities of capitalism are destroyed by common failings.

Sachs, Jeffrey D. *The End of Poverty: Economic Possibilities for Our Time.* New York: Penguin Books, 2005. Perhaps no economist has been more influential to the course of economic policy making and poverty alleviation around the world than Jeffrey Sachs. This book discusses the varied approaches that are necessary to rid the world of profound poverty and defends the proposition that doing so is possible in the near future.

Smith, Adam. *An Inquiry into the Nature and Causes of the Wealth of Nations.* New York: Collier Press, 1909. The most important work in the history of economic thought. Smith touches on virtually every subject that defines the scope of modern economics. This is an essential text for everyone.

Yergin, Daniel, and Joseph Stanislaw. *The Commanding Heights.* New York: Touchstone, 1998. This is the definitive catalog of economic thinking and ideological battles of the 20th century.

**Notes**